FIELD GUIDE
TO BRITISH

BIRDS
GARDEN & COUNTRYSIDE

FIELD GUIDE TO BRITISH
BIRDS
GARDEN & COUNTRYSIDE

ROBERT BURTON

Colour plates by
TIM HAYWARD

Contents

Colour Plates
Tim Hayward

Illustrations
Pages 8-26 Aziz Khan

First published in 1982 by
Octopus Books Limited
59 Grosvenor Street, London W1

© 1982 Hennerwood Publications
Limited

ISBN 0 7064 2090 X

Produced by
Mandarin Publishers Ltd
22a Westlands Road
Quarry Bay, Hong Kong

Printed in Hong Kong

Introduction

A total of 498 species of wild birds has been seen in the British Isles, and the number is increasing every year. Of these, 298 have nested here within the last ten years and more than 100 visit regularly on migration. The remainder are 'accidentals' which are seen only very rarely; they have been carried well outside their normal range by some freak of weather. The increasing number of birds on the 'British list' is due to the growing ranks of bird-watchers. Recording a rare bird is a technical process; the description has to be accepted by a panel of experts. For most of us the pleasure of bird-watching comes from recognizing and observing the common birds.

Eighty-three birds have been chosen for this book. They include most of the common species seen in the open countryside or in gardens, which are an extension of the countryside reaching into built-up areas. A few are less familiar, like the corncrake and wryneck, and often they are, regrettably, becoming rare. Nevertheless, the selection is a cross-section of the variety of birdlife of gardens and countryside. There is a good chance that a strange bird will be similar to one described and illustrated in the book, so this will help to establish its identity.

It is impossible to list exactly what birds may be seen in any particular place. Every bird has a habitat where it feeds and nests but some, like the chaffinch, blackbird, wren and starling, live almost everywhere. Others are found only in a special habitat, such as the

swans on lakes and rivers, but the power of flight makes birds very mobile and they can turn up in unlikely places. They may have been blown off course, or they may be passing through on migration. A few have even been carried across the Atlantic Ocean; the first myrtle warbler, an American species, to be seen in Britain was found in a garden. So, when using this book, remember that many birds are not included, even though they could be spotted in gardens, countryside or even the centre of towns. The peregrine, for instance, is an inhabitant of wild mountains and sea-cliffs but it has nested in city centres. It seems that high-rise buildings are an acceptable substitute for a cliff-face.

The birds are arranged in the accepted international order of classification, and this will become familiar as the book is used. It will soon be possible to find a bird quickly by looking in the right section of the book. For a start, it can be seen immediately that waterbirds are at the beginning and songbirds at the end. Finding out about a bird is made easy because all the information is given on a single double-page spread. Its identity can be checked with the illustration and the written description of its plumage. Once it has been named, its habits can be watched. For each bird, basic information is given on feeding, nesting and migration, together with where and when it is likely to be seen. The main text which accompanies the data describes any points of interest.

Watching birds

Watching birds, whether as a serious hobby or merely enjoying their visits to the birdtable, is one of the most popular pastimes. No special knowledge is needed. Patience and a good eye are the basic necessities for birdwatching, but enjoyment is much greater if you buy some simple equipment.

The most useful item is a pair of binoculars. They should be tried out at the shop and certain points looked for. The best size for everyday use is 8 x 30; the first figure is the magnification, the second is the diameter of the larger lenses. A higher second figure gives a better light-gathering power and the binoculars will give a brighter image in dim light. The binoculars should be focused by a central wheel, which should revolve easily, and there must be a separate adjustment for one eyepiece so that the binoculars can be adjusted for your eyes. They should focus down to about 5 metres (16 feet).

The second necessity is a notebook in which to record observations for reference later. It is not a good idea to try to identify a bird by thumbing through a bird book at the time. Write down a description to compare with details in the book and make a sketch. It does not matter if the drawing is very rough, so long as it shows the shape of bill, wings and so on, and the position of the colours. Try to compare the bird with one you already know.

Photographing birds is a specialized pastime, but good results can be obtained by positioning a camera on a tripod near a birdtable or birdbath and using a long pneumatic shutter release from a hiding place. Photographing nests should be avoided because of the disturbance it causes, and it is illegal to photograph some birds at their nests.

It is easy to draw a bird if the illustration is built up in pieces. Smooth the outline and add details of plumage. The method can be used for different postures.

Notes of what you see are essential reminders of past observations. Make notes of behaviour, such as a flock of starlings bunching when attacked by a hawk, and build up a picture of the bird's way of life.

Studying behaviour is a useful way of identifying birds and learning how they live. Some birds (below) have a very distinctive way of flying, while others can be observed as they feed. The treecreeper and nuthatch feed from tree trunks; the treecreeper always climbs upwards but the nuthatch can descend head first.

Dunnock

Chaffinch

Treecreeper

Nuthatch

Plumage and moulting

Identifying an unknown bird is easier if the different parts of its plumage are known. Details of its appearance can be noted quickly and they are helpful when describing what you have seen to another birdwatcher. Some of the fine details are not needed if the bird has plain plumage but, for some species, details of plumage may reveal whether it is male, female or juvenile.

The three main parts of the plumage which need to be described are the body, the wings and the tail. Each needs to be inspected carefully for small features, such as coloured tips to the tail or wing feathers, or a stripe above the eye. They may be more important for identification than larger areas of coloration.

Feathers gradually become worn in everyday use and have to be replaced by moulting. Most birds moult their feathers once a year. It is not easy to tell when the moult is taking place unless gaps can be seen in the wings and tail as a bird flies overhead. The gaps show where feathers have been shed and new ones are growing.

Occasionally a bird changes colour at its moult. A familiar example is the male mallard which loses its bright colours after the breeding season, then regains them in a second moult at the end of summer. A few birds change colour when their feathers wear. The brambling appears brown in winter until the tips of the feathers wear off to reveal the glossy black summer plumage underneath.

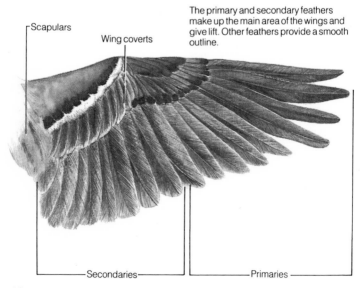

Scapulars

Wing coverts

The primary and secondary feathers make up the main area of the wings and give lift. Other feathers provide a smooth outline.

Secondaries

Primaries

Each part of a bird's plumage has a name. Knowing these names helps when describing an unknown bird.

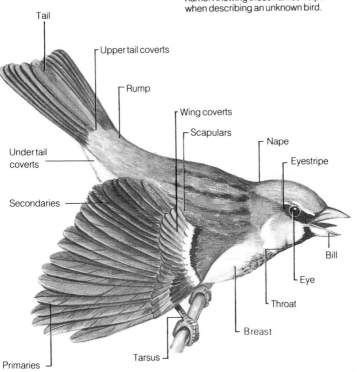

Tail

Upper tail coverts

Rump

Wing coverts

Scapulars

Nape

Eyestripe

Under tail coverts

Secondaries

Bill

Eye

Throat

Breast

Primaries

Tarsus

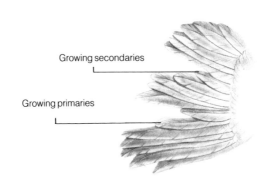

Growing secondaries

Growing primaries

Design for flight

The mastery of the air has called for many changes in the bodies of birds. Apart from the transformation of the arms into wings for propelling the bird through the air, the entire skeleton has become stronger and lighter. The bones are hollow and thin but have a network of struts inside to combine this lightness with strength. The number of bones has been reduced, as in the short tail and the replacement of teeth with a horny bill, which may also be used as a hand. However, the neck has more vertebrae than in other animals

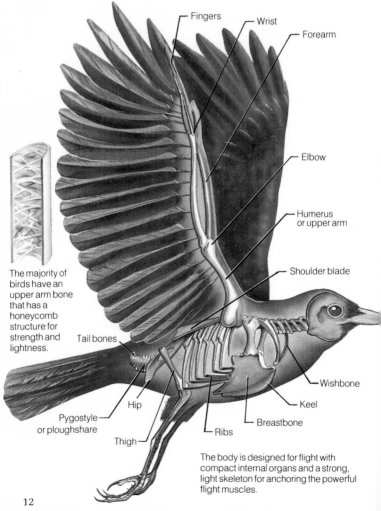

Fingers

Wrist

Forearm

Elbow

Humerus or upper arm

Shoulder blade

The majority of birds have an upper arm bone that has a honeycomb structure for strength and lightness.

Tail bones

Wishbone

Keel

Hip

Pygostyle or ploughshare

Thigh

Ribs

Breastbone

The body is designed for flight with compact internal organs and a strong, light skeleton for anchoring the powerful flight muscles.

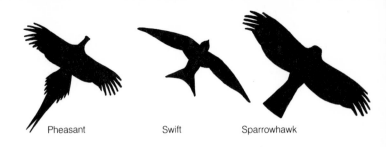

Pheasant   Swift   Sparrowhawk

and is very flexible to facilitate feeding and preening. The collar-bones are fused to make the 'wishbone' which braces the wings.

The plumage, or covering of feathers, is a unique feature of birds. The vane of the feather is a marvellously strong and light construction of filaments held together with minute hooks. Feathers have two main functions. They keep the bird warm by trapping a layer of air next to the body, in the same way as the fur of a mammal. They also streamline the body and provide the main surface area of the wings and tail. Underneath the outer covering of feathers, there is a layer of inner down feathers for extra insulation.

As with aircraft, lift is provided by air flowing over the wings. The bird does not 'row' through the air; the primary feathers go through a figure of eight motion pushing the bird upwards and forwards. The power for flight is provided by huge breast muscles which are attached to the deep 'keel' on the breast bone. If human beings had wings, a chest 2 metres (6½ feet) deep would be needed to accommodate the muscles needed to fly. The breast muscles are attached to the wing bones by tendons and cause the wings to beat up and down, while other muscles alter the position and shape of the wings in a complicated sequence during each wingbeat. The downstroke is the main powerstroke for propelling the bird. As the wings are pressed down to provide lift, the primary wing feathers bend and act as a propeller so that the bird is thrust forwards. On the upstroke the wings still provide lift and thrust, because they are twisted, and the primary feathers open and bend back so that each acts as a separate propeller. Finally at the top of the upstroke, the wings flick fully open and add a little more propulsive effort. Steering is effected by adjustments to the wings, so that one produces more thrust, and by using the tail as a rudder.

A bird's flying ability is related to the shape of its wings and tail. High-speed birds, like the swift, have long, slender wings. The swallow is a fast flier but its long tail feathers enable it to manoeuvre well at low speed. The sparrowhawk has broad wings and a long, square tail which are needed for high-speed twisting and turning through trees and the precisely controlled pounce on its prey. The pheasant's broad, short wings give it the lift needed for vertical take-off in dense woodland while the long tail helps it to steer between the branches.

13

Naming birds

Birds have different names in various languages and sometimes even have several names in one country. To avoid confusion they are given scientific names which are used internationally. The scientific name also shows how one bird is related to others. The system of scientific names was devised by the Swedish naturalist Linnaeus more than 200 years ago. He used Latin and sometimes Ancient Greek names because these were international languages.

Robin

Blue tit

Rook

Mallard

Bullfinch

A species of bird comprises all the individual birds of one kind which can breed with each other but not with other species. Robins breed with other robins but never with sparrows or starlings. A group of similar species is called a genus and the scientific name shows the genus, followed by the species. The carrion crow is *Corvus corone*. The genus name *Corvus* is Latin for crow. The closely related rook is *Corvus frugilegus* and the jackdaw is *Corvus monedula*. The magpie is in a separate genus: *Pica pica*. However, it is sufficiently closely related to be placed in the same family of birds – the crow family, Corvidae. Other families are built up in the same way.

When two slightly different birds can interbreed, they are said to belong to different subspecies. Carrion and hooded crows have the same habits but can be distinguished by plumage and they sometimes mate and rear offspring. The scientific name of the carrion crow is *Corvus corone corone* and the hooded crow is *Corvus corone cornix*.

The ten families shown on this page are a small sample of the 36 families which contain the 83 species described in this book and there are 56 families in the complete list of British birds. The largest

Wood pigeon

Swallow

Green woodpecker

Pheasant

Dunnock

family in Britain is the duck family Anatidae, which includes the geese and swans. Forty two species have been recorded in Britain. On the other hand, the wren and the nightjar are the only British members of the families Troglodytidae and Caprimulgidae.

Some bird families are easy to distinguish. No one could confuse a duck with a pheasant, but others are not so obvious. Swallows and martins belong in the family Hirundinidae but the swifts, which look rather similar and also hunt flying insects, are in the family Apodidae. Placing a bird in its family depends more on the detailed structure of its skeleton rather than on its external appearance. For instance, it seems strange on outward appearances that ducks, geese and swans belong to one family, while the barn owl is given its own family, Tytonidae, separate from the other owls (Strigidae family) on the basis of anatomical differences not visible in the field.

Many common birds of garden and countryside, which belong to several families, share two important characteristics. They are called the perching birds or song birds. Their toes are arranged so that they can easily grip a perch and most of them produce melodious songs.

Breeding

Birds start their preparations for rearing families at the beginning of spring. Some have spent the winter near last year's nesting place; others have gathered in flocks which now split up again. Some time later the migrants will return from warmer countries. The males usually show breeding behaviour first. They claim an area of ground as a territory which they defend against other males of their species and attract females so that they can pair up. Possession of a territory enables the pair to court, build a nest and rear a family without disturbance. The territory may also be an exclusive feeding ground.

The territory may be defended in a number of ways. The presence of the owner is often sufficient to keep trespassers out but he may have to threaten them. A robin threatens rivals by showing off its red breast to best advantage. The intruder feels insecure when he is trespassing and usually retreats so that actual fighting is rare. Ownership of a territory is often advertised by song. These melodious sounds which are so pleasing to the human ear have a vital function. The song is not only a warning to other males but also a welcome to unattached females. They are often delivered from favoured perches or in 'song-flights' which mark out the extent of the territory.

Once a female has been attracted, the male proceeds to court her. Courtship often consists of showing off the plumage in displays. These may be spectacular in the case of mallards and great crested grebes. When the pair has become established the birds maintain the bond between them by continuing to display, and many birds, including jackdaws, pigeons and herons, preen each other. The male may feed the female during both courtship and incubation.

Great-crested grebes court with a succession of ritual displays, which show their bright plumage.

Mallard drakes often display together to attract the ducks

Male blackbirds can be seen bowing to and then chasing rivals

Nesting

The nest is a cradle for the eggs and young birds. They are kept together where the parents can keep them warm and the young are looked after until they can fend for themselves. Nests of some sort are used by many fishes, amphibians, reptiles and mammals but are a speciality of the birds.

Some birds make little or no nest. The nightjar and the stone curlew lay their eggs on the bare ground, the tawny owl and kestrel lay their eggs on ledges or in disused nests of other birds, and the cuckoo lays in occupied nests, leaving the rightful owners to rear its offspring. At the other extreme there are the elaborate domed nests of the wren and the long-tailed tit, and the laboriously excavated cavity nests of woodpeckers and the kingfisher. In general, elaborate nests are employed by birds whose young are helpless at hatching. These birds are called nidicolous, meaning 'nest-staying'. Simple nests are usually made by birds whose young are nidifugous, meaning 'nest-leaving'. They hatch in an advanced state of development and can run or swim within a few hours.

The most familiar birds' nests are the neatly constructed cups built by garden and woodland birds, such as the blackbird, chaffinch and dunnock. A few build a dome over the top for added protection; for instance the magpie, wren and house sparrow. Although the nest cup looks as if it has been woven, the method of construction is more like making felt. The bird works the nest material together by sitting on the foundations and slowly rotating, while it pushes with its breast and tramples with its feet. A lining of softer feathers, hair or fine grass is usually added after the cup has been completed.

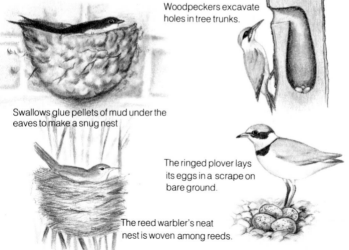

Woodpeckers excavate holes in tree trunks.

Swallows glue pellets of mud under the eaves to make a snug nest

The ringed plover lays its eggs in a scrape on bare ground.

The reed warbler's neat nest is woven among reeds.

Adapting to nature

Bills. The main function of a bird's bill is to collect food and each species has a bill which is adapted to a particular diet. By examining a bird's bill it is possible to guess what it eats and how it gets its food.

The song thrush eats a wide range of animal and plant foods and its bill is a universal tool for grabbing, hammering and grasping. It can dig holes in the soil to extract grubs or pull out a resisting worm, pluck a berry, pick up crumbs and smash a snail against a stone. Members of the crow family, such as the carrion crow, rook and jackdaw, have similar unspecialized bills and they also have a sense of curiosity which leads them to prod anything which might yield a meal.

Other birds have, in general, become specialists. The wood-peckers, for example, use their bills for chiselling into wood to extract grubs. The construction of their heads is designed to reduce the shock of the hammer blows. Yet, despite this specialization, woodpeckers are adaptable enough to feed on fruit and nuts or to rob birds' nests.

The birds illustrated on this page show a range of bills. The shoveler sifts a multitude of tiny animals from the water, while the heron stalks and stabs individual fish. The kestrel kills and tears its prey and the bullfinch crushes seeds. The nightjar and the blue tit are insect-eaters but with very distinct habits. The nightjar scoops up flying insects in its huge gaping mouth; the blue tit not only uses its slender, tweezer-like bill for picking tiny insects off leaves or pecking

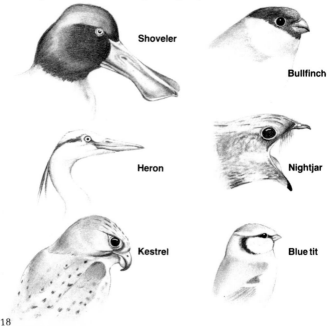

Shoveler

Bullfinch

Heron

Nightjar

Kestrel

Blue tit

seeds, but it also deals with large caterpillars, drills holes in pine cones to extract grubs and tears milk bottle tops to get at the cream. Nevertheless, its small bill is basically for picking up tiny insects as is the smaller bill of the warblers.

The finches have short, stout conical bills for cracking seeds, and each species has a slightly different bill for a different diet. The hawfinch has a hefty bill which can crack cherry stones in contrast to the goldfinch's slender bill which is used for extracting and splitting the soft seeds of dandelions and thistles.

Feet. Most birds have four toes; three pointing forwards and one backwards. Running birds, like partridges, have strong legs and a very short back toe, but walking birds, such as the skylark, have a long claw on the back toe. Birds which spend their time in trees and bushes hop rather than walk, even when on the ground. When they are perching, the toes curl round. As the bird bends its legs, tendons pull the toes tight and clamp the bird firmly to the perch.

Variations in feet are shown by the birds of prey which have strong toes with sharp talons, and the waders which have well-spaced toes for walking on soft sand or mud. Water birds, such as ducks and geese, have webbed feet or fleshy lobes around each toe, as do the grebes and coots. Woodpeckers have two toes facing forwards and two facing backwards to give a good grip on tree trunks.

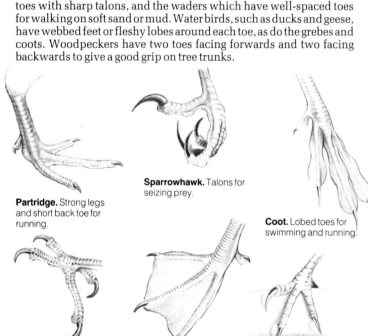

Partridge. Strong legs and short back toe for running.

Sparrowhawk. Talons for seizing prey.

Coot. Lobed toes for swimming and running.

Woodpecker. Two toes forward, two back for clinging to tree trunks.

Mallard. Webbed feet for swimming.

Blackbird. Curled toes for perching.

Movement and migration

The power of flight gives birds the ability to travel long distances with ease, and many birds move about in search of the best places to feed. Swifts, for instance, fly away from approaching rainstorms which make catching flying insects difficult. Every morning in winter flocks of starlings fly out of city centres in search of food, returning to roost at night. Their commuter journeys change as new supplies of food are found and old ones are used up.

Bird movements may be spectacular. Some species suddenly 'irrupt' in large numbers, leaving their native homes and flying to faraway places. These irruptions are caused by a sudden shortage of food. Snow and frost in northern and central Europe may cut off food supplies so that blackbirds, ducks, starlings and others flee to the milder weather of western and southern Europe, including Britain. The most spectacular irruptions are seen when waxwings, siskins, bramblings or crossbills arrive in large numbers because of the failure of the crops of seeds on which they depend. Some birds are called partial migrants because some members of a population are resident while others travel away for the winter. In Scandinavia most chaffinches fly south and the number which stay behind depends on the severity of the winter. However, in Britain, very few chaffinches move south.

True migration is the regular, twice-yearly movement between two

Summer visitors

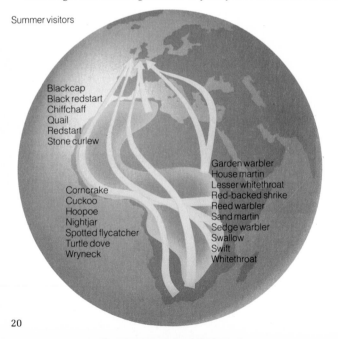

Blackcap
Black redstart
Chiffchaff
Quail
Redstart
Stone curlew

Corncrake
Cuckoo
Hoopoe
Nightjar
Spotted flycatcher
Turtle dove
Wryneck

Garden warbler
House martin
Lesser whitethroat
Red-backed shrike
Reed warbler
Sand martin
Sedge warbler
Swallow
Swift
Whitethroat

areas. It is a means of escaping a shortage of food in winter. When the insect-eating swallows, swifts and warblers have flown south to the warmer climates of Africa, other birds arrive in Britain for the winter. Redwings and fieldfares fly in from Scandinavia, while geese and waders come down from their Arctic nesting grounds. Some stay for only a short time before continuing their journey southwards.

The two main mysteries of bird migration are how a bird knows when to start its journey and how it knows where to go. A true migrant starts its journey before there is a shortage of food and it has to build up reserves of fat to sustain it during the flight. It is born with the instinct to migrate and the signal to prepare for the journey involves the change in day length, the weather and other factors. If the summer has been good, birds may leave early because they have built up their food reserves quickly. Weather conditions can affect the birds' arrival at their destination. They can be held up or blown off course by contrary winds.

Migrant birds also have an instinctive knowledge of where to fly. They steer a course with the aid of sun or stars. They also seem to have the navigator's equivalent of sextant, chronometer and charts in their heads so that they can calculate where they are and which way to head. Some birds can sense the Earth's magnetic field, like a compass, and keep on course even when the sky is hidden by clouds.

Winter visitors

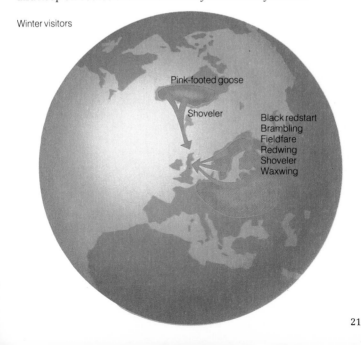

Pink-footed goose

Shoveler

Black redstart
Brambling
Fieldfare
Redwing
Shoveler
Waxwing

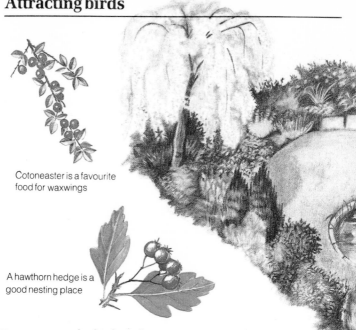

Cotoneaster is a favourite
food for waxwings

A hawthorn hedge is a
good nesting place

For some people, birdwatching is an excuse to visit wild places. Others like to attract birds into their gardens where they can be watched in comfort. The ultimate luxury is to have a huge floor-to-ceiling window overlooking one's garden, which preferably has a pond. On a more modest scale, birds can be attracted to any garden by putting out food and, with some planning, a proper bird garden can be organized. First, it is important to recognize that birds require three basic essentials: food, water and safe shelter for roosting and nesting. A garden which is manicured by weeding, trimming and mowing is not very attractive to birds, but a compromise between neatness and a varied habitat for birdlife can easily be achieved.

Many common garden birds originate in woodland. They have taken to living in gardens because this environment has similarities to a wood, where there are four layers of vegetation: open ground and grass, herbs, shrubs and trees.

Blackbirds and thrushes search for food in open flowerbeds and lawns while wrens and dunnocks like the shelter of bushes. Lawns attract parties of starlings which probe busily for worms, pied wagtails which sprint after insects and, occasionally, a green woodpecker searching for ants.

Herbaceous borders and shrubberies provide food either as flowers and seeds or harbour insects which the birds like. Sparrows may wreak havoc by tearing up crocuses, but goldfinches make a welcome

Ivy provides
cover and food

Dense bushes of laurel are
safe roosting places

sight when they feed on the seeds of Michaelmas daisies, thistles and groundsel.

Shrubs and trees which bear berries are very attractive to birds. Blackberry thickets, hawthorn hedges and elder trees are native species which give good crops of fruit, although many people prefer to pick them for their own use rather than leave them for the birds. Cotoneaster is especially favoured by waxwings when they arrive in winter. Privet is unsatisfactory if it is well clipped but, if allowed to grow through the summer, produces tiny delicate flowers and black fruits which birds like. It also makes a good nesting place. Clumps of rhododendrons and bamboos are popular roosts for sparrows.

Trees are needed for nesting places by some birds; a large tree may attract a pair of owls. Evergreen holly and yew provide plenty of cover and berries to eat. In late winter and spring, male birds start to sing on the bare branches. This is a good time to learn their songs because the birds are easy to see and identify. At the end of the year, fallen fruits are eagerly devoured by thrushes and blackbirds.

A pond is an asset to any garden. It can be simply made from an old sink or by lining a hole with thick polythene. A covering of wire-netting is useful in autumn to catch falling leaves. A shallow area or a sloping rock gives the birds a place to drink and bathe. Even small ponds may attract a heron, although its visits will not be appreciated if the pond is stocked with goldfish.

Birdtables and nestboxes

Hanging nut dispenser

Covered birdtable

Birdtables and nestboxes are easy to make at home and they encourage birds to use the garden. There is no need to buy expensive timber as scraps of wood are adequate, provided they are sound, and only a basic skill in carpentry is needed to produce satisfactory results.

The simplest birdtable consists of a platform nailed or screwed to a post, or slung from a bough. If space is limited, the table can be fixed to a bracket outside the window. The table should be about 1.5 metres (5 feet) above the ground to deter cats leaping on to it and to prevent dogs reaching up to steal food. The platform is best made from a solid board rather than plywood which is liable to warp and split. A raised strip around the sides prevents the food from blowing off, but a gap should be left so that the table can be cleaned and for rain water to drain away. A roof helps to keep the food dry but is not essential.

The birdtable is likely to receive few visitors in the summer when there is plenty of natural food, but a continuous provision of food through the winter will ensure the survival of many small birds which would otherwise succumb to hard weather. Bread and other kitchen scraps make acceptable offerings but peanuts and proprietary bird foods are especially welcome. Scraps should be crumbled so that starlings and crows cannot carry away too much. Tits and greenfinches soon learn to use hanging feeders; the plastic-mesh bags in which onions and oranges are sold are ideal for this. Strangely, siskins are particularly attracted by orange or red bags. A favourite

24

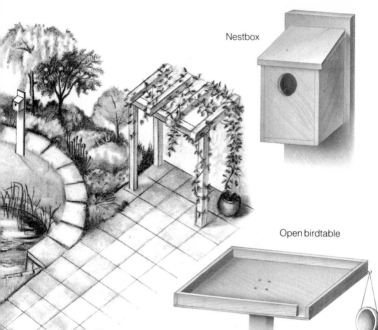

Nestbox

Open birdtable

with tits is a half coconut shell suspended on a string and filled with molten fat mixed with scraps – scrapings from the frying pan for example. Finally, do not forget birds like dunnocks which forage on the ground. Scatter some of the provisions for them as well.

The basic nestbox, popular with tits, tree sparrows and nuthatches, is a straightforward construction which has a sloping roof with an overhang at the front. A hinge with fastening clasps or brass screws enables the lid to be removed for cleaning out after the nesting season. An entrance of 2.8 cm (1⅛ in) diameter prevents sparrows ousting tits. There should be plenty of room – a front height of 20 cm (7⅞ in) and a floor 12 x 12 cm (4¾ x 4¾ in). Old floorboards have the right dimensions as well as the necessary thickness for durability and keeping the interior snug. The box must be weatherproof and positioned to avoid the worst wind and rain and the hottest sun. Sandwich a sealing compound between the joints during construction to make them waterproof and drill a drain hole in the floor. A second sort of nestbox has an open front and is favoured by robins and blackbirds.

It is too late to put up nestboxes when the birds have started courting and nest-building. They should be in place during the autumn because some birds start to prospect for likely nesting sites during the winter months and, in fact, they have been known to use nestboxes for roosting before breeding in them.

How to use this book

Each double-page spread gives the details needed to identify a species of bird, together with further information on its habits and where it can be found. All 83 species of birds depicted on the following pages can be seen in gardens and parks or in the open countryside of farmland, heaths and commons. Some are familiar; others are less well known or even rare. Unknown birds can be identified by using the hints for identification given on pages 8-9 and searching through the illustrations and plumage descriptions. Scientific terms used in the descriptions are included in the glossary on page 190.

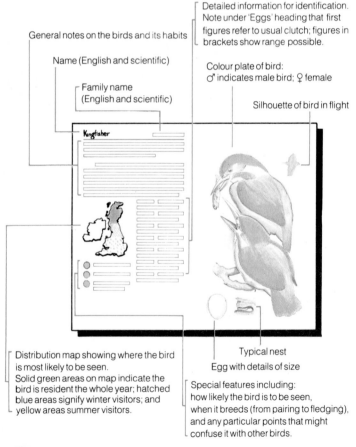

General notes on the birds and its habits

Name (English and scientific)

Family name
(English and scientific)

Detailed information for identification. Note under 'Eggs' heading that first figures refer to usual clutch; figures in brackets show range possible.

Colour plate of bird:
♂ indicates male bird; ♀ female

Silhouette of bird in flight

Kingfisher

Distribution map showing where the bird is most likely to be seen.
Solid green areas on map indicate the bird is resident the whole year; hatched blue areas signify winter visitors; and yellow areas summer visitors.

Typical nest
Egg with details of size

Special features including:
how likely the bird is to be seen,
when it breeds (from pairing to fledging),
and any particular points that might confuse it with other birds.

FIELD GUIDE TO BRITISH

BIRDS
GARDEN & COUNTRYSIDE

Little Grebe
Tachybaptus ruficollis

Although the little grebe (or dabchick) is a common waterbird it is often overlooked because it spends much of its time skulking in dense waterside vegetation. It is found in farm ponds, swamp pools, weed-fringed canals and ornamental lakes, as well as in disused gravel pits and hill tarns and lochs; in fact in any still or slow-moving water where there are plenty of water plants. It can survive on stretches of water where boats and human activities drive many of the other birds away.

The little grebe lacks the ornate head plumage of the great-crested grebe and does not have elaborate display rituals. Its presence is often revealed by a pair's trilling duets. The nest is a pile of water plants in the water and the adult hides the eggs by pulling vegetation over them as it leaves. The young are sometimes carried on the parent's back and may remain there when it dives.

○ Frequent.

○ Resident.

○ Breeding, March-September.

○ Sexes similar.

○ Water rail has red bill, white undertail coverts and slender body.

○ Great-crested grebe larger, with eartufts and frill.

○ Coot is black with white shield on head.

○ Moorhen has red shield and flicks tail as it walks.

Plumage: Dark brown with chestnut on neck and face. Short, whitish tail, from rear. Distinctive pale yellow patch at base of bill. Winter plumage is paler; the chestnut turns to buff. Juvenile lacks yellow patch and has dark streaks on side of head. Length 27cm (10½ in).

Voice: Shrill trill, and a soft, whistling alarm note.

Habitat: Slow and still waters with plenty of cover.

Food: Water snails and insects, small fish, crustaceans and amphibians.

Nest: A floating pile of vegetation among water plants, built by both sexes.

Eggs: 4-6 (2-7). White, staining to brown. April-July. Usually two clutches. Incubated for 20 days by both sexes.

Young: Nidifugous. Fed by both parents for 30-40 days. Fly at 44-48 days.

In the field: Secretive habits. A squat, rounded body, blunt at rear. Flies with legs trailing. Yellow patch at base of bill.

juvenile

adult

38 mm

Great-crested Grebe
Podiceps cristatus

Like all grebes, the great-crested grebe has a short tail and legs placed at the rear of the body. When it comes ashore it stands upright, like a penguin. The toes have fleshy lobes to assist swimming. At one time rare through persecution for its fine feathers, the great-crested grebe is now widespread in Britain, except for northern Scotland. It breeds on lakes and slow rivers, preferring those 3-4 metres (10-13 feet) or less deep, and it has taken advantage of the many newly excavated gravel pits. Outside the breeding season, most great-crested grebes move to coastal areas and estuaries.

In the early part of the year, pairs of great-crested grebes perform spectacular courtship displays, including 'head shaking', the 'cat-attitude', in which the birds swim with wings half spread, and the 'penguin dance', where they face each other, standing erect in the water, during which the frill and eartufts are raised.

- Frequent.

- Resident.

- Breeding, February-October.

- Sexes similar.

- Divers similar in flight but they lack wing patches.

- Little grebe is smaller.

Plumage: Back dark brown; underparts white. White patches on leading and trailing edges of wings seen in flight. In breeding season, distinct chestnut and black frill and black eartufts; only reduced eartufts present in winter. Juvenile lacks eartufts and has white face with black streaks. Length 48 cm (19 in).

Voice: Shrill repeated bark; also guttural and groaning calls.

Habitat: Still fresh water. Also salt water in winter.

Food: Small aquatic animals and some plants.

Nest: A pile of water plants, sometimes afloat, among reeds or other cover in shallow water. Built by both sexes.

Eggs: 3-4 (1-9). White, staining to brown. May-July. Usually one brood. Incubated for 28 days by both sexes.

Young: Nidifugous. Fed by both parents. Fly at 9-10 weeks. Dive at 6 weeks. Often carried on parent's back.

In the field: Distinct frill and eartufts. In flight, long drooping neck, trailing legs.

♂ summer

♂ winter

55 mm

Grey Heron
Ardea cinerea

Usually called simply 'the heron' because no other species is commonly seen in Britain, the grey heron is a familiar sight wherever there is water. It nests in colonies, called heronries, usually in tall trees but sometimes in reedbeds or on cliffs. Once a heronry is established the birds return year after year. The nests are fortified with extra material each season until they become totally unstable and are blown down.

There is no mistaking a heron either on the ground or flying with slow beats of its broad, arched wings. When not standing motionless, a heron is usually seen stalking slowly forwards in shallow water, ready to shoot out its neck to grab a fish or frog with its sharp bill. They sometimes hunt on land and may become unpopular when they raid fish farms or steal goldfish from garden ponds. This habit makes herons an unexpected 'garden bird'.

◉ Common.

◉ Resident.

◉ Breeding, February-August.

◉ Sexes similar.

◉ Bittern is very secretive with brown, mottled plumage.

◉ Night heron is smaller, with a short neck and black mantle.

◉ Spoonbill is white with flat, spoon-shaped bill.

Plumage: Mainly grey with white on the head and underparts, black flight feathers and streaks on throat. Black stripes run through eyes to the crest which normally dangles like a pigtail. The dagger-shaped bill is yellow but becomes reddish in spring. Juveniles are more uniformly grey and have short crests. Length 91 cm (36 in).

Voice: Loud, harsh *frarnk*.

Habitat: Areas with shallow stretches of water including city parks. Also found at mountain lakes and on the coast.

Food: Mainly fish, but also frogs, rodents, birds and many kinds of freshwater insects, crustaceans and molluscs.

Nest: A platform of twigs which may become very large. Built by female with material brought by male.

Eggs: 4-5 (1-10). Pale blue. February-April. Second clutch is rare. Incubated for 25 days by both sexes.

Young: Nidicolous. Fed by both parents. Fly at 50 days. Return to nest for 10-20 days.

In the field: Large size, long neck and legs, grey coloration.

juvenile

adult

60 mm

Mute Swan
Cygnus olor

This is the largest British bird and it is one of the best known. Mute swans were domesticated in medieval times because they were good to eat. All mute swans belonged to the Crown or to privileged people and institutions who were given the right of ownership. The swan's owner was shown by a pattern of notches on the bill. Catching and marking swans, called 'swan-upping', is still carried out along the River Thames.

Mute swans are not as silent as their name suggests. Flocks of swans can be heard grunting and hissing to each other. Neither are swans as dangerous as is sometimes said. The male drives away other swans and threatens people by arching his wings and curving his neck.

Swans fly with their necks outstretched and their powerful wing-beats produce a musical beating note. They usually land on water where they can splash down and use their feet as brakes.

○ Common.

○ Resident.

○ Breeding, April-October.

○ Male rather bigger and with larger knob on bill, especially in breeding season.

○ Bewick's and whooper swans hold their necks more erect and have yellow bills.

Plumage: All white. The bill is orange with a black knob at the base, which is larger in the male. The juvenile is dirty grey with a brown bill. Length 152 cm (60 in).
Voice: A quiet grunting and hissing. A louder snort when threatened.
Habitat: Any stretch of water large enough for take-off, and with plenty of water plants for food. Also in estuaries.
Food: Water plants, sometimes frogs, water snails, insects and fish.
Nest: A large pile of vegetation near water. Built by female with the male bringing material. Lined with a little down.
Eggs: 5-8 (1-11). White with a grey tinge. April-June. Incubated for 36 days by the female, but male takes over when she is feeding.
Young: Nidifugous. Tended by both parents. Male looks after older young (cygnets) until the rest hatch. Sometimes ride on parent's back. Fly at 4½ months.
In the field: Huge white bird with long neck and orange bill.

juvenile

adult

115 mm

Canada Goose
Branta canadensis

The Canada goose is a native of North America and those living in Britain are descendants of American geese brought across the Atlantic three centuries ago. In Victorian times Canada geese were kept in parks but as their numbers increased, they have taken to living wild. They now live in many parts of England and Wales, and less commonly in Scotland and Ireland.

Like other species of goose, the Canada goose mates for life. The gander (male) drives away intruders by advancing with neck stretched horizontally and hissing. When he returns to his mate, the pair indulge in a 'triumph ceremony' in which they wave their necks in a sinuous movement and give a special 'triumph-note'. This ceremony is also used when the male and female meet after a period of separation. The family stays together throughout the winter and the young geese are chased away at the start of the next nesting season.

○ Frequent.

○ Resident.

○ Breeding, April-July.

○ Sexes similar, but male rather larger.

○ Barnacle goose is smaller and black and grey, with more white on head.

Plumage: Body is grey-brown, paler on the breast and underparts and white under the tail. Head and neck are black, with a white patch on the side of the face, from the chin to behind the eye. The tail is black and contrasts with the white upper-tail coverts. Length 97 cm (38 in).

Voice: Trumpeting *ah-honk*.

Habitat: Unlike other geese, it lives inland, on and around lakes, gravel pits, slow rivers and marshes.

Food: Mainly grass, and some water plants.

Nest: A pile of grass or reeds near water, often on an island. Lined with down.

Eggs: 5-6 (2-11). White. April-May. Incubated for 28-30 days by female with male standing guard.

Young: Nidifugous. Tended by both parents. Fly at six and a half weeks.

In the field: A large goose, brown-bodied with black neck and white on head. In flight, shows a white chevron on the tail.

86 mm

Pink-footed Goose
Anser brachyrhynchus

GEESE, SWANS AND DUCKS
Anatidae

The pink-footed goose spends the summer in the Arctic. It nests on the tundras of Greenland, Iceland and Spitzbergen and migrates south as the first frosts of the Arctic winter start. Geese from Greenland and Iceland fly to the British Isles and those from Spitzbergen head for Denmark, the Netherlands and Germany.

British pink-footed geese gather at traditional grounds, mainly in Scotland, where they are counted every year. Numbers have been increasing because changes in farming have given them more food in the winter. The geese graze on pastures, stubble and potato fields, and cereal crops, and are sometimes unpopular with farmers because of damage caused to pasture and growing crops. After spending the day in feeding, the flocks fly to roost on estuaries, lakes or reservoirs. They choose places where they will be safe and they now prefer reservoirs to the traditional estuary roosts, where wildfowlers wait for them.

○ Scarce.

○ Winter visitor.

○ British Isles, October-April.

○ Does not nest in British Isles.

○ Male slightly larger.

○ Greylag goose lacks contrast between body and neck and has large yellow bill.

○ White-fronted geese have white at base of bill, orange legs and dark bars on breast.

○ Bean goose has orange legs and orange and black bill.

Plumage: Head and neck dark brown, body grey-light brown with pink tinge and transverse white bars on back. Upper tail-coverts white, tail grey with white tip. Bill pink and black. Feet pink. Length 71 cm (28 in).
Voice: Musical, honking *ang-ank*.
Habitat: Farms. Roosting on estuaries and inland waters.
Food: Grass, fallen grains, potatoes and other crops.
Nest: Low mound of vegetation on open ground. Built by female.
Eggs: 3-5 (1-9). White. May-June. Incubated 26-27 days by female with male on guard nearby.
Young: Nidifugous. Tended by both parents. Fly at 56 days and stay with parents throughout winter.
In the field: Short-necked goose with dark head and neck and pale upperparts. Small pink and black bill. Pink feet and legs.

79 mm

Mallard
Anas platyrhynchos

Found in almost every part of the country, the mallard is the ancestor of domestic ducks and it becomes tame very easily. For most of the year, the gaudy plumage of the male (the drake) contrasts with the dull browns of the female (the duck) but from July to September the males moult into the 'eclipse plumage' and become almost the same colour as the females. The sexes can still be distinguished by the male's yellow bill. Courtship and pairing start in autumn. Although basically monogamous, the drakes often try to mate with any duck.

Mallards eat a variety of plant and animal food which they find both on land and on water. When they feed on the water surface they rapidly pump water in and out of the mouth and edible particles are trapped in a fringe of plates on the edge of the bill. This is called 'dabbling'. Food is found underwater by 'upending' or diving.

○ Common.

○ Resident.

○ Breeding, March-June.

○ Male more brightly coloured than female for most of the year.

○ Teal is small, has green speculum.

○ Shoveler has white and chestnut body and distinctive broad bill.

Plumage: Male has an iridescent green head and neck, with a white collar, brown breast and grey-brown back and underparts. Tail coverts are black, with two feathers curled upwards. The tail is white. The female is brown, as is the male when in 'eclipse'. Both sexes have a purple speculum edged with black and white. Juvenile is similar to female. Length 58 cm (23 in).

Voice: The familiar loud quack is made by the female. The male's call is a quieter rasp.

Habitat: Any small or large stretch of water; spends much of time nearby. Also on moorland, estuaries and coasts in winter.

Food: Land and water plants, acorns, seeds and small animals.

Nest: Dead leaves lined with down, made by female, on the ground but sometimes in trees or old buildings.

Eggs: 9-13 (4-18). Greyish-green. Usually March. There may be a second clutch if the first is lost. Incubated by female for 28 days.

Young: Nidifugous. Led to water by female. Male may remain nearby. Fly at 7-8 weeks.

In the field: Purple speculum. Green head of male.

♂

♀

57 mm

Shoveler
Anas clypeata

The shoveler is immediately distinguished from other ducks by the spoon-shaped bill from which it gets its name. The edges of the upper and lower halves of the bill are fringed with fine plates, rather like the teeth of a miniature comb. When feeding, the shoveler holds its bill agape so that the plates intermesh to form a sieve. Water is pumped in and out of the mouth and food is trapped in the sieve. The mallard often feeds in the same way but its plates are not so well developed as those of the shoveler.

Shovelers can only find sufficient food in waters which are teeming with small floating life. This means that shovelers are found mainly in the lowland parts of Britain. They are rare in Wales, the West Country and northern Scotland, and are most abundant in the marshes and fens of East Anglia and Kent.

Shovelers are migratory. Those breeding in Britain winter in southern Europe and are replaced by more northerly immigrants.

○ Scarce.

○ Summer and winter visitor.

○ British Isles, March-November.

○ Breeding, April-July.

○ Male boldly coloured.

○ Mallard lacks white and brown.

○ Shelduck has much more white.

Plumage: Male has dark green head, white neck, breast and scapulars, chestnut flanks and belly, and blackish back. Female has light and dark brown patterning like female mallard. Male similar outside breeding season. Both sexes show pale blue forewing in flight. Juvenile resembles female. Length 51 cm (20 in).

Voice: Male has quiet clucking and wheezing notes; the female louder quacks.

Habitat: Fertile shallow water, with reeds etc, marshes, fens and sewage farms.

Food: Small swimming crustaceans ('water fleas'), insects and fishes; molluscs and floating plant seeds.

Nest: Grass and down-lined hollow in a low cover built by female.

Eggs: 9-11 (6-14). Buff to olive. April-June. Incubated for 22 days by female.

Young: Nidifugous. Tended by female. Fly at 6 weeks.

In the field: Large bill and pale blue forewing.

52 mm

Tufted Duck
Aythya fuligula

The tufted duck is one of the most numerous British ducks and the only one to have a drooping crest at the back of the head. Like the mallard, it takes advantage of man-made waters and its numbers have increased recently, perhaps because freshwater mussels, its favourite food, are abundant in the new gravel pits and reservoirs. Tufted ducks are particularly easy to see on reservoirs and large lakes in winter where they may gather in large flocks. However, they prefer places with plant cover for breeding. Several females may nest together on one island and they often nest in colonies of gulls or terns, which give the ducks protection from predators.

Unlike the mallard, the tufted duck regularly dives in search of food and can stay under for as long as 40-50 seconds (although it is more usually less than 20 seconds). It prefers to feed in depths up to 3 metres (10 ft). Tufted ducks 'up-end' in shallow water and may come ashore to feed. Like most diving ducks they have to patter along the water's surface before taking off.

○ Common.

○ Resident.

○ Breeding, April-August.

○ Male distinguished by black and white plumage.

○ Scaup is a very similar duck appearing in winter but male has grey back and female has distinct white patch at base of bill (female tufted duck sometimes has a little white here).

Plumage: The male is black, with a green gloss, except for the white flanks and belly. It has an inconspicuous drooping crest on the back of the head. From July to September it has an eclipse plumage in which the white flanks are lost. The female is dark brown with white on the belly which disappears in summer. It has a very small crest. Juvenile is similar to female. Length 43 cm (17 in).

Voice: Male has a quiet whistle. Female has a harsh growl.

Habitat: Lakes and ponds, often coming into parks. Also estuaries in winter.

Food: Water snails and insect larvae. Some water plants.

Nest: Depression in ground lined with reeds and down, made by female.

Eggs: 8-11 (3-22). Green-grey. May-June. Incubated for 23-28 days by female.

Young: Nidifugous. Tended by female until they can dive. Fly at 6 weeks.

In the field: Male black and white, crested. Both sexes have long white wing bar in flight.

♀

♂

58 mm

Sparrowhawk
Accipiter nisus

The sparrowhawk remained a common bird of prey despite persecution by gamekeepers and farmers, but it eventually succumbed to chemicals in the 1950s. The chemicals were used to protect crops from insect pests and were taken up by insect- and seed-eating birds, such as sparrows, finches and tits. These birds form the main prey of sparrowhawks, so the poisons were passed on and accumulated in the hawks' bodies. The use of these chemicals is now controlled and sparrowhawk numbers are increasing.

Sparrowhawks are fast, agile fliers. They hunt by flying low through woods or along hedges and taking their prey by surprise. They sometimes hunt around buildings. The flight is of three or four wingbeats followed by a long glide. A sparrowhawk may keep watch from 30 metres (100 ft) up, then dive to the ground with wings half-folded. Prey is taken to a perch or 'plucking post' which becomes conspicuous as remains gather under it.

○ Frequent.

○ Resident.

○ Breeding, April-August.

○ Male smaller with rufous underparts.

○ Goshawk is considerably larger but plumage is very similar.

○ Kestrel hovers, has pointed wings and streaked underparts.

Plumage: Male is grey above and white with rufous bars below. The much larger female is brown above with brown bars below. Both sexes have broad transverse bars on the tail. Juvenile is brown above with broader barring below. Length 28-36 cm (11-14 in).

Voice: Rapid *kew-kew-kew-kew* and whistling *whee-oo*.

Habitat: Farms with hedges, and gardens, or wherever there are trees.

Food: Mainly small birds, up to ducks and grouse, also some small mammals and insects.

Nest: Sticks and leaves, sometimes laid on the old nest of a pigeon, crow, jay etc.

Eggs: 4-6 (3-7). Bluish-white with dark brown markings. Late April-May. Incubated for 35 days by female who is fed by male.

Young: Nidicolous. Male brings food which female gives to young. Later, female also hunts. Fly at 26-28 days.

In the field: Long tail, rounded wings and low, rapid flight. Barred underparts.

♂

♀

40 mm

Kestrel
Falco tinnunculus

The kestrel is the most common British bird of prey, and has become a familiar sight along motorways where it hovers over the verges in search of mice, voles and beetles. Other birds can hover with a good wind to assist them, but the kestrel, which used to be called the windhover, has made a speciality of this method of hunting. In a strong wind, a kestrel can hover without flapping its wings and the head is kept absolutely steady while the body moves around it. This makes it easier for the kestrel to spot the slight movements of its prey. Typically, the kestrel hovers for a short time, then glides downwind and hovers again while it scans a new patch of ground.

Like other falcons, the kestrel does not build a nest. It uses a rock ledge, a hollow tree or the old nest of another bird. Kestrels are now becoming familiar in towns where they nest on buildings and prey on sparrows.

○ Common.

○ Resident.

○ Breeding, March-August.

○ Male has grey on head and tail, female has barred tail.

○ Sparrowhawk has rounded wings and barred underparts.

○ Merlin smaller, darker above and no moustachial stripe.

○ Cuckoo has unmistakable call, very pointed wings, club-shaped tail and fine barring underneath.

Plumage: Male has chestnut upperparts, marked with black spots. Head, rump and tail grey, with black band and white tip on tail. Underparts buff with dark spots. Female is brown above with black bars which are fine on the back and broad on the tail. Paler below. Both sexes have a black moustachial stripe or 'tear streak' under the eye. Juvenile resembles female. Length 33-36 cm (13-14 in).

Voice: Shrill *kee-kee-kee*.

Habitat: Found in nearly every kind of countryside, including seacliffs, open woods and moors.

Food: Mainly mice and voles, insects, especially beetles, and some small birds, occasionally earthworms.

Nest: On ledges, in hollows or forks in trees or in old nest of other bird. No nest material.

Eggs: 3-6 (1-9). White with dark brown blotches which may almost cover the egg. April to June. Incubated for 28 days, mostly by female who is fed by male.

Young: Nidicolous. Male brings food at first, later both feed young. Fly at 27-32 days.

In the field: Pointed wings, slim tail and habit of hovering.

♀

♂

40 mm

Grey Partridge/Red-legged Partridge

Perdix perdix/Alectoris rufa   Phasianidae

The common partridge is sometimes referred to simply as 'the partridge' but it is more often called the grey partridge to distinguish it from the red-legged or French partridge which was introduced from France 200 years ago. The native grey partridge is found over most of Britain, except north-west Scotland and west Wales, but the red-legged partridge is found mostly south and east of a line running from the Tees to the Exe. This is the drier part of the country and the red-legged partridge does not flourish in areas of high rainfall.

Partridges have become less abundant in recent years largely because the removal of hedges destroys their nesting places, and autumn ploughing, pesticides and late springs destroy the insect food which is necessary for the survival of the chicks.

Grey partridge   Red-legged partridge

○ Common.

○ Resident.

○ Breeding, April-June.

○ Male grey partridge has chestnut mark on breast. Red-legged partridge: sexes similar.

○ Quail much smaller and paler.

○ Pheasant has long tail.

Plumage: Chestnut head, grey neck and underparts. Back and flanks chestnut with darker barring. Male has inverted dark chestnut patch on breast. Juvenile lacks chestnut colouring and barring. Length 30 cm (12 in). (Red-legged partridge: Brown upperparts with grey on crown. Breast grey, shading to brown underneath. Red tail seen in flight. Juvenile similar to young grey partridge. Length 34 cm (13½ in).)
Voice: Grating *krrr-ik*. (Red-legged partridge: a harsh *chuck-chuck-or*.)
Habitat: Farmland with hedgerows.
Food: Mainly leaves and seeds, but chicks eat mostly insects.
Nest: Hollow in the ground lined with grass, under hedges. Made by female.
Eggs: 9-20. Olive brown. (Red-legged partridge: 10-16. Yellowish-white with red spots.) April-May. Incubated for 23-25 days by female.
Young: Nidifugous. Tended by both parents. Fly at 16 days, before fully grown. (Red-legged partridge: Fly at 23 days.)
In the field: Plump bird, which stretches its neck when disturbed. Runs rapidly or flies low with alternate fast wingbeats and glides.

Red-legged partridge

Grey partridge

adult

adult

Red-legged partridge

Grey partridge

41 mm

36 mm

Quail
Coturnix coturnix

The quail is the smallest of the European gamebirds and the only one to migrate. It flies south in the autumn to spend the winter in Africa, south of the Sahara. In some years the British population rises sharply because warm weather and favourable winds draw more quails northwards into the British Isles.

Despite being a gamebird, and so attracting the attention of sportsmen and gamekeepers as well as naturalists, the habits of the quail are not well known. It is very secretive and its small size enables it to slip unnoticed through standing corn and thick herbage. When flushed, quails fly low and fast, and soon drop back into cover. The best way of discovering their whereabouts is to listen for the characteristic *wet-my-lips* call.

○ Scarce.

○ Summer visitor, sometimes staying for winter.

○ British Isles, April-October.

○ Breeding, May-July.

○ Male distinguished by dark neck band.

○ Partridges are larger but quail are easily confused with their juveniles.

Plumage: Yellow-brown with dark brown and black streaks on head and back. Rufous underneath with pale streaks on flanks. Conspicuous patterning on head, and male has a dark neck band, lacking in female. Juvenile like female but barred rather than streaked. Length 18 cm (7 in).
Voice: Loud, staccato, repeated call, described as 'wet-my-lips'.
Habitat: Rough grass and cereal crops, especially on chalk downland.
Food: Seeds and insects.
Nest: Shallow hollow with plant lining, built by female.
Eggs: 8-13 (7-18). Creamy-white with brown spots. May-June. Sometimes two clutches. Incubated 17-20 days by female.
Young: Nidifugous. Tended by female. Fly at 19 days and stay together as a 'bevy' for further 1-2 months.
In the field: Small, plump bird with short tail, slipping through vegetation. Distinctive call.

♂

♀

30 mm

Pheasant
Phasianus colchicus

Originally a native of the south-eastern corner of Europe and parts of Asia, the pheasant was spread across Europe by the Romans and they probably brought them to Britain. Pheasants have been a privileged gamebird, protected by law, for 150 years and they are most abundant where artificially reared and protected by gamekeepers. However, they also live wild where they have escaped from the preserves.

Pheasants are commonly seen in fields and open country but they need tall hedgerows and spinneys to provide cover for nesting and perches for roosting. In winter, they are likely to retire to the greater shelter of woodlands.

The broad stubby wings and long tail are used for an explosive almost vertical take-off when a pheasant is disturbed. The noisy rattle of the wingbeats confuses predators and alerts other pheasants.

○ Common.

○ Resident.

○ Breeding, April-July.

○ Female smaller and drab.

○ Partridges and other gamebirds are much smaller and have short tails.

Plumage: Male is brilliantly coloured. The head and neck are dark green above a white ring. The bare patch around the eye and 'eartufts' is red. Body and tail are chestnut with black scalloping and barring. There are also varieties with almost black or pale body plumage. The female is a drab buff with dark scalloping and barring. Juvenile is like the female. Length 71-91 cm (28-36 in).

Voice: Harsh, loud *kork-kok*, used as a territorial call and repeated rapidly as an alarm.

Habitat: Farms and parks. Also woodland.

Food: Seeds, fruit and small animals found by scratching the ground.

Nest: Shallow depression in the ground.

Eggs: 8-15 (2-25). Olive or brown. April-June. Incubated for 23-28 days by female.

Young: Nidifugous. Tended by female. Fly at 12 days. Independent at 70-80 days.

In the field: Long tail, and glossy plumage of male. Some, but not all, have white neck-ring.

♀

♂

46 mm

Water Rail
Rallus aquaticus

Although the water rail lives in many parts of the country, it is one of the less familiar birds. It skulks in dense vegetation on the edge of water and rarely comes into the open like its familiar relatives, the coot and moorhen. Its main home is in beds of reeds and osiers, swamps and the overgrown edges of lakes, old canals and gravel pits, where there is dense aquatic vegetation, and muddy ground.

The drab coloration makes the water rail very difficult to spot, particularly when it remains stock still, and the body is flattened from side to side, so that it can slip through the densest vegetation without disturbing it. As a result, the best way of finding water rails is to listen for their calls. These have been described as 'heart-rending and fearsome groans' or as sounding 'like a dying pig', and they are known by the old Norfolk name of 'sharming'.

○ Frequent.

○ Resident.

○ Breeding, March-August.

○ Sexes similar.

○ Young moorhen uniformly coloured and lacks barred flanks; shorter bill.

○ Little grebe uniformly rufous above; shorter bill.

Plumage: Greenish-brown with black streaks above, grey below. Flanks barred with black and white. Undertail coverts whitish. Long red bill. Juvenile grey with dark bars underneath. Length 25 cm (10 in).

Voice: Grunts and squeals.

Habitat: Areas of water with overgrown borders and muddy places.

Food: Insects and other invertebrates; occasionally amphibians, fish, seeds and fruit.

Nest: Cup of dead leaves on ground near water. Built by both sexes.

Eggs: 6-11 (5-16). White with spots. April-July. 2 broods. Incubated 20 days by both sexes.

Young: Nidifugous. Tended by both parents. Fly at 20-30 days.

In the field: Long red bill. Grey underparts and white bars on flanks.

36 mm

Corncrake
Crex crex

At one time the corncrake was a common bird of the British country-side. Although it was rarely seen its rasping call, which led to both the English and scientific names, was a familiar sound on summer evenings. The call resembles the noise of a ratchet on a fishing reel rattling as an angler pulls out his line. It can be imitated by running the teeth of a stiff comb over the edge of a block of wood.

The corncrake's name is misleading since it does not inhabit corn fields but prefers hayfields and damp meadows with rank growth of nettles and low weeds. As agriculture expanded in the 19th century, the pastures and hayfields offered new homes for corncrakes and their numbers rose. However, modern agriculture is against them; the old pastures are disappearing and mechanical hay-cutting performed earlier in the year often destroys the nests, and the corncrake is again becoming rare.

○ Scarce.

○ Summer visitor.

○ British Isles, April-October.

○ Breeding, May-August.

○ Sexes similar.

○ Water rail has long bill and grey underside.

○ Quail is smaller with patterned head.

○ Partridge has red head; gregarious.

Plumage: Uniform buff and red-brown with dark mottling on the back and chestnut wing coverts. Vertical bars on flanks. Blue-grey on face. Length 28 cm (11 in).
Voice: A repeated, rasping *crake-crake*.
Habitat: Hayfields, meadows, crops such as potatoes.
Food: Insects and small invertebrates; some shoots and seeds.
Nest: Well concealed shallow cup lined with leaves. Sometimes domed.
Eggs: 8-12 (6-14). Dull green with brown or grey spots. May-July. Incubated for 18 days by female.
Young: Nidifugous. Tended by female. Fly at 35 days.
In the field: Call. Chestnut wing-coverts.

37 mm

Moorhen
Gallinula chloropus

The moorhen's name comes from 'mere' meaning a lake. It is an amphibious bird, more at home on land than most waterbirds. It swims well but it is also a strong runner and climbs trees. The moorhen's feet are not webbed and the toes are very long. It floats high in the water, yet it can dive well and if danger threatens may hide underwater with only the bill showing.

Moorhens always live near water, although they may be found wandering several hundred metres from the nearest stretch. They prefer water surrounded by trees and other vegetation and moorhens living on lakes keep to sheltered parts of the shore. The sharp call from dense cover often betrays their presence.

The family life is unusual. Moorhens raise two or three families each year and the older chicks help look after their younger brothers and sisters. They feed them, brood them and help to repair the nest if it is damaged by floods.

○ Common.

○ Resident.

○ Breeding, March-September.

○ Sexes similar.

○ Coot has white shield.

○ Water rail is grey and brown with long, slender bill.

Plumage: Dark grey, brown and black, paler underneath. A white line along the flanks and white undertail coverts. Waxy-red shield at base of bill. Juvenile brown with pale chin. Length 33 cm (13 in).
Voice: Sharp *kurr-uk*.
Habitat: Ponds, lakes and slow rivers with plenty of plant cover.
Food: Wide variety of leaves, seeds, fruits and small animals, obtained from water or land. May raid birds' nests.
Nest: A large cup of stems and leaves among water plants or in tree. Built by both sexes.
Eggs: 5-9 (2-13). Buff with brown spots. March-April for first clutch. 2-3 clutches. Incubated for 21-22 days by both sexes.
Young: Nidifugous. Fed by both parents. Fly at 40-50 days. Independent at about 70 days.
In the field: Black with red shield. Constant flicking of tail shows white coverts. Smaller than coot.

juvenile

adult

44 mm

Coot
Fulica atra

Compared with its relative the moorhen, the coot prefers larger stretches of still water. Flocks of several hundred gather on lakes, gravel pits and reservoirs in winter. They form dense groups which keep away from the banks, although they will roost and feed on land but do not move far from water. The toes bear flat lobes which act as paddles when swimming but are not such a hindrance as fully webbed feet when running.

Coots are argumentative birds. Pairs defend their territories, which they may hold all the year, and scuffles often break out among the flocks when birds come too close. Squabbles are accompanied by much splashing. The aggressor runs across the water on its lobed feet, with the assistance of flapping wings and the two race off together leaving a trail of splashes. If neither bird will retreat, they face each other, rearing up and lashing out with their feet and bills.

○ Common.

○ Resident.

○ Breeding, March-August.

○ Sexes similar.

○ Moorhen has red shield and bill and white on tail.

○ Water rail is grey and brown with long slender bill.

Plumage: Black with slight green gloss and white shield and bill. Juvenile more brown and pale on throat and face, lacking white shield. Length 38 cm (15 in).
Voice: A loud high-pitched *kowk*.
Habitat: Lakes, reservoirs, urban ponds, gravel pits, slow rivers and sometimes in sheltered estuaries.
Food: Leaves and seeds of plants and small animals. Steals food from other birds.
Nest: Large cup of stems and leaves in shallow water. Built by both sexes.
Eggs: 6-10 (1-13). Buff with black specks. March-May. Sometimes two clutches. Incubated for 21-24 days by both sexes.
Young: Nidifugous. Cared for by both parents, who may divide brood between them. Fly at 55-60 days.
In the field: Black with white shield and bill.

juvenile

adult

53 mm

Stone Curlew
Burhinus oedicnemus

The stone curlew is the only British representative of the family which otherwise live in warmer parts of the world. It is found in Europe, North Africa and eastwards to India. Britain is, therefore, at the north and west of its range and there are only a few areas where it can find its favoured habitat. Stone curlews like open, dry ground so they are found on chalk downs, sandy heaths and occasionally shingle banks and sand dunes. Such areas are being increasingly cultivated or planted with trees leaving less room for stone curlews.

The pale plumage of the stone curlew makes it difficult to find, particularly as it spends the day lying quietly out of sight and becomes active only in the evening. If disturbed it is likely to 'freeze', flattened to the ground, rather than fly. Stone curlews are active throughout the night, when their loud wails and whistles make an eerie chorus.

○ Rare

○ Summer visitor.

○ British Isles, March-October.

○ Breeding, April-August.

○ Sexes similar.

○ Curlew has long, curved bill.

○ Ringed plover much smaller with black stripes on head.

Plumage: Sandy buff with dark brown streaks; paler on throat. A white bar on the wing is revealed as two bars when in flight. Length 41 cm (16 in).

Voice: A shrill *coor-lee*, like a curlew, with many other whistles and cries.

Habitat: Downs, heaths and shingle beds. Also fields and firebreaks in plantations.

Food: Slugs and snails, worms, insects. Occasionally small birds and mammals.

Nest: Eggs laid on bare ground.

Eggs: 2 (1-3). Yellowish-brown with dark brown spots and streaks mainly at blunt end. April-May. Incubated for 26 days by both sexes.

Young: Nidifugous. Tended by both parents. Fly in 40 days.

In the field: Calls. Large yellow eyes. White wing bars. Large round head.

54 mm

Ringed Plover/Little Ringed Plover

Charadrius hiaticula/Charadrius dubius

PLOVERS

Charadriidae

The ringed plover is a bird of the shores which now nests increasingly inland, on shingle banks of upland rivers and by reservoirs and gravel pits. After breeding, our native ringed plovers retire to muddy and sandy shores where they are joined by migrants from the Arctic.

The single *tooli* note of alarm is often the first indication of a ringed plover's presence. This means that the bird's territory has been invaded and, if the nest or crouching chicks are approached too closely, the plover starts its 'distraction display' to lure you away. It either runs past with one wing held low or flapping, or it runs directly away with its tail fanned. The bird makes itself very conspicuous.

The little ringed plover first nested in Britain in 1938 and has now spread over much of England, where it has made use of man-made reservoirs and gravel pits.

Ringed plover   Little ringed plover

- ◯ Scarce.
- ◯ Resident.
- ◯ Breeding, March-July.
- ◯ Sexes similar.

Plumage: Brown with white underneath and distinct black collar; white collar above and black band over eyes. In flight: white patch on each side of the tail and a fine white wing bar. Juvenile like adult but scaly appearance on back and black bands less conspicuous. Length 19 cm (7½ in). The little ringed plover is similar but the legs are pink; there is no wing band and the bill is darker. A white line above the head band. Length 15 cm (6 in).
Voice: Liquid trilling song and *tooli* note. Little ringed plover has similar song and a *teeoo* note.
Habitat: River banks, reservoirs, gravel pits. Also sea shores. Little ringed plover found more inland.
Food: Insects, winkles, small crustaceans and worms.
Nest: A shallow scrape sometimes lined with plants or pebbles.
Eggs: 4 (3-5). Buff with brown-black blotches. May-July. Incubated for 24-25 days by both sexes.
Young: Nidifugous. Tended by both parents. Fly at 25 days.
In the field: Black and white markings on head. Call.

Little ringed plover

Ringed plover

Little ringed plover 30 mm
Ringed plover 36 mm

Black-headed Gull
Larus ridibundus

The black-headed gull is the gull mostly likely to be seen inland. It is found over most of the country, although it rarely breeds inland in the southern counties. The colonies may contain hundreds or thousands of pairs, and are situated in marshes, reedy shallows of lakes, gravel pits and sewage farms. Coastal colonies are usually on sand-dunes and saltmarshes. Small parties stream from the colony to feeding grounds along the shore, in towns and on farmland, where the gulls cluster behind the plough.

The black-headed gull is one of the birds which have benefited from the changes which have been made to the countryside over the last 100 years. This has resulted in its taking advantage of the increase in arable land and rubbish dumps for food, and new lakes and sewage farms for nesting and roosting. It often follows the plough to feed on animals exposed in the newly turned soil. In towns, black-headed gulls forage on scraps.

○ Common.

○ Resident.

○ Breeding, April-July.

○ Sexes similar.

○ Herring and common gulls have pure white head and yellow bill.

○ Mediterranean and little gulls have no black on wing tips.

Plumage: Body white, the wings grey with black tips. White line on underside of wing. In summer the head acquires a chocolate brown 'hood' and the bill and legs become red. In winter the head is white with dark patches over the ear and in front of the eye; the bill and legs are orange. Juvenile mottled brown. Length 36 cm (14 in).

Voice: Harsh, shrieking *kwar*.

Habitat: Farmland, marshes, urban parks, reservoirs, rivers; also low coasts, estuaries, hills and moors.

Food: Plants and small animals, including garbage.

Nest: Rough saucer of plant material. Built by both sexes.

Eggs: 3 (2-6). Buff to brown with dark brown flecks. April-May. Incubated for 22-24 days by both sexes.

Young: Nidifugous. Fed by both parents. Fly at 5-6 weeks.

In the field: Colour of head and legs, although black head disappears outside breeding season. White line under black-tipped wings.

♂ winter

♂ summer

52 mm

Feral Pigeon
Columba livia

The pigeons which infest city squares, parks, railway stations and other urban areas are descendants of the rock dove which nests in sea caves. As with the swallow, rock doves found that buildings are good substitutes for caves and took to nesting in human habitations. Eventually special dovecotes were built and the pigeons became semi-domesticated. They fed in the fields and their young were taken for food. The fast flight and habit of returning to a familiar roost led to the development of homing and racing pigeons.

About 150 years ago after the Agricultural Revolution and the improvement of food supplies, dovecotes fell into disuse and the pigeons had to fend for themselves. They now nest on buildings in towns, on ruins and on seacliffs, where they intermingle with rock doves. So much interbreeding has taken place that it is now difficult to decide which are pure rock doves without any feral pigeon blood.

○ Common.

○ Resident.

○ Breeding, all year.

○ Sexes similar.

○ Rock dove has longer bill.

Plumage: Blue-grey with white rump and undersides of wings (the 'blue'); sometimes with black spots on wing coverts (the 'blue chequer').
Others range from pure white to pure black through a variety of colours and patterns. Length 33 cm (13 in).
Voice: Purring *ooo-croo*.
Habitat: Towns, cities, villages and farmland. Also coastal cliffs.
Food: Seeds and scraps.
Nest: Twigs and grass arranged in hole or on a ledge. Built by female.
Eggs: 2 (1). White. Year round in towns. Average 5 clutches. Incubated for 17 days by both sexes.
Young: Nidicolous. Fed by both parents. Fly at 4-5 weeks.
In the field: Varied colouring distinguishes most feral pigeons.

juvenile

adult

31 mm

Stock Dove
Columba oenas

DOVES AND PIGEONS
Columbidae

There is no real difference between doves and pigeons. The former is Norman-French, the latter Anglo-Saxon. 'Dove' is, however, usually given to smaller species. The stock dove's name comes from an old word for a tree trunk or stem (as in rootstock) and refers to the dove's habit of nesting in hollow trees.

The stock dove was originally a bird of open woodland and it hardly ever feeds away from the ground. Nowadays, it is most common on farmland and in parks. It is often overlooked because of its similarity to the wood pigeon but is distinguished by its gruffer call.

Many plant-eating birds feed their young on insects to give them the protein they need for growth but doves and pigeons feed their young on a protein-rich substance which is secreted from the crop. The young pigeons or squabs get this 'pigeon's milk' by thrusting their heads down the parent's throat.

○ Common.

○ Resident.

○ Breeding, March-October.

○ Sexes similar.

○ Wood pigeon has white patches on wings and neck.

○ Rock dove has white rump.

○ Turtle and collared doves have brown back and black and white collar.

Plumage: Darker bluish-grey than the wood pigeon. Upperside of wings pale with dark trailing edge. Rear part of tail black. Glossy green patches on neck. Throat and breast dark pink. Juvenile duller, lacking green patches. Length 33 cm (13 in).

Voice: Deep, repeated *ooo-eroo*.

Habitat: Farmland, parks. Also woods and sea cliffs.

Food: Mainly plant food including crops. Occasionally small animals.

Nest: Usually a hole in a tree or in a building or cliff, with little or no lining. Rarely among branches or under bushes.

Eggs: 2 (1-3). White. March-September. 2, sometimes 3 clutches. Incubated for 17 days by both sexes.

Young: Nidicolous. Fed by both parents. Fly at 26 days.

In the field: Pale, black-bordered tail and wings. Lacks white markings.

adult

juvenile

38 mm

Wood Pigeon
Columba palumbus

As the name suggests, the wood pigeon was once a forest bird, but as much of our forestland has disappeared over the years it has adapted well to living in towns and on farms. Unfortunately the wood pigeon's ability to survive has turned it into a pest; gardens are raided for peas and cabbages, and farms supply grain and other crops. Winter crops such as clover and young greens are ravaged by large flocks of pigeons and farmers find the increasing numbers are difficult to control. When not provided with easy pickings from fields and gardens, wood pigeons feed in trees. They can clamber through the foliage with surprising agility and even hang upside down to get at the last acorns, beech mast or buds.

The familiar soft cooing is the male's song. He also makes his presence known with display flights: flying up and gliding down, while 'clapping' his wings. The claps are made by a 'whiplash' beat of the wings, not by striking together. Wood pigeons 'burst' noisily from cover when disturbed.

○ Common.

○ Resident.

○ Breeding, March-October.

○ Males often have larger white neck patches and pinker breasts than females.

○ Stock dove lacks white on neck and wing.

○ Turtle dove and collared dove have brown back and black and white collars.

○ Rock dove has white rump.

Plumage: Bluish-grey, darker on the wings; black primaries and rear half of tail. Breast pinkish turning white on belly. White edge on wings becomes a bar in flight. White patch on side of neck edged with glossy green and purple. Juvenile lacks white patch on necks. Length 41 cm (16 in).

Voice: A *coo-coo-coo, coo-coo.*

Habitat: Farms, gardens, parks, woodland, and sometimes hills and coasts.

Food: Mainly vegetable, including crops, bread and other scraps, nuts and berries. A few worms, snails, slugs and insects.

Nest: A slightly built cup of twigs. Eggs can often be seen through the bottom. Female builds; male gathers material.

Eggs: 2 (1-3). White. Mainly August-September. 3 clutches. Incubated for 17 days by both sexes.

Young: Nidicolous. Fed by both parents. Fly at about 35 days.

In the field: White patches on neck. White wing bar.

juvenile

adult

41 mm

Collared Dove
Streptopelia decaocto

The collared dove nested for the first time in Britain as recently as 1955 and has been officially declared a pest. The original home of the collared dove was in the south-eastern corner of Europe but, in about 1930, it started an explosive spread across the continent. By 1938 it had reached Austria. Germany was colonized in 1943 and then the dove started across France in 1952. Eventually it even nested as far north as Iceland.

It is not known why the collared dove suddenly started to spread, but colonization of its new homes was made easy because its way of life did not bring it into competition with other birds. It lives around human habitations and takes advantage of spilt grain around farms, docks, mills and so on. This supply is available all the year round and the doves may breed through the winter. During the summer, families overlap as squabs are still being fed while the next clutch is being incubated.

○ Common.

○ Resident.

○ Breeding, March-October.

○ Sexes similar.

○ Wood pigeon has white patches on wings and neck.

○ Stock dove is grey with green patches on neck.

○ Turtle dove has chequered upperparts; white belly.

○ Rock dove has white rump.

Plumage: Light grey with dark primaries and tail, and brown back and wing coverts. Edges of tail pale. Underside of tail white with black base. Black and white collar. Juvenile greyer, lacks collar. Length 32 cm (12½ in).

Voice: A monotonous *coo-coo-coo*, with the stress on the second *coo*. In flight a harsh *kwurr*.

Habitat: Farms and gardens. Usually absent from town centres and open country.

Food: Mostly grain picked from ground. Rarely berries and small animals.

Nest: A flimsy cup of twigs on a tree or wall, well hidden. Built by both sexes.

Eggs: 2 (1-3). White. Mainly March-September. Up to 5 clutches. Incubated for 15 days by both sexes.

Young: Nidicolous. Fed by both parents. Fly at 16 days.

In the field: Long, white-edged tail, black-and-white underneath. Lands after a 'bouncing' run-in.

juvenile

adult

30 mm

Turtle Dove
Streptopelia turtur

The turtle dove's name comes from the Latin *turtur* which describes this species' purring call. It is smaller and slimmer than other common pigeons and often seen in pairs or small parties. The turtle dove's favourite habitat is open ground with trees or shrubs where it can both feed and nest, or roost. This makes farmland ideal and, like stock doves and wood pigeons, turtle doves have become much more common in the last one or two centuries. The distribution of the turtle dove in Britain is further linked with the availability of fumitory, a common weed of arable fields and waste places. Between one-third and one-half of the turtle dove's diet consists of fumitory seeds.

The turtle dove's breeding season is shorter than those of most doves which extend to the end of summer or later. This is because it is a migrant. By the end of July, nesting comes to an end and the doves moult their body feathers and build up fat reserves for the flight to Africa.

○ Common.

○ Summer visitor.

○ British Isles, April-October.

○ Breeding, May-July.

○ Sexes similar.

○ Wood pigeon has white patches on wings and neck.

○ Stock dove grey with green on neck.

○ Collared dove has plain brown on back.

○ Rock dove has white rump.

Plumage: Head and body generally dark grey with conspicuous rufous, black spotted back and wing coverts. Tail black with white on each side of tip. Breast pink, belly white. Black and white striped patch on neck. Juvenile lacks patch on neck. Length 28 cm (11 in).
Voice: Deep, repeated purring.
Habitat: Farmland, parks and large gardens.
Food: Mainly seeds of fumitory and other weeds. Also grain, some leaves and small animals.
Nest: Flimsy platform of twigs in hedge or bramble. Built by both parents.
Eggs: 2 (1-3). White. May-July. 2 clutches. Incubated for 14 days by both parents.
Young: Nidicolous. Fed by both parents. Fly at 20 days.
In the field: Rufous and black chequered back. Black tail with white at corners.

adult

adult

39 mm

Cuckoo
Cuculus canorus

The cuckoo's call is familiar to everyone but the bird itself is often overlooked and is easy to confuse with a sparrowhawk or kestrel. It usually arrives from Africa in mid-April and males start calling immediately to attract a mate.

After mating the female searches for the nests of other birds where she will lay her eggs. She chooses one with an incomplete clutch, lays her own egg in it and removes one of the others. The cuckoo parasitizes many kinds of small birds but the most frequent are the meadow pipit, reed warbler and dunnock.

As soon as it has hatched, the nestling cuckoo sets about ejecting the host's eggs and nestlings from the nest until it is alone and can command its foster parents' full attention.

Adult cuckoos leave the country and fly back to Africa before the young cuckoos, which must rely entirely on instinct to guide them to their destination.

○ Common.

○ Summer visitor.

○ British Isles, March/April-July/August (Juveniles to September).

○ Breeding, March/April-June.

○ Female rather brownish.

○ Sparrowhawk has rounded wings.

○ Kestrel lacks barring and hovers.

Plumage: Upperparts and breast blue-grey. Underparts white with grey bars. Upper surface of tail spotted with white. Juvenile brownish above, with white spot on nape. Length 33 cm (13 in).

Voice: Far-carrying *cuckoo* call by male. Chuckle by female.

Habitat: Farmland with trees. Also woods, moors and hills.

Food: Insects, especially caterpillars, moths and butterflies, and grubs of flies and beetles. Young are fed on the diet of their foster parents.

Nest: None. Eggs are laid in the nest of another bird.

Eggs: About 12, one in each nest. Variable colouring, including blue, brown and green shades with brown or grey markings. May-June. Incubated for 12½ days.

Young: Nidicolous. Reared by foster parents. Fledge at 3 weeks.

In the field: Call. Pointed wings and long club-shaped tail. Grey above and barred below.

juvenile

adult ♂

23 mm

Barn Owl
Tyto alba

Pale and ghostly in flight, white-spotted, orange-buff and white when seen at close quarters, the barn owl is one of Britain's most beautiful birds. Unfortunately it is becoming rare; it lives on farmland and picks up toxic chemicals through its diet of rodents. In addition, old barns and trees are disappearing so that this owl is deprived of places to roost and nest.

Although they hunt mainly at night, barn owls can often be seen in the evening as they fly along regular paths, at a height of only a few metres. During the nesting season, when there is a brood of hungry chicks, the owls are forced to hunt by day.

Barn owls locate their prey by vision and hearing. Laboratory experiments have shown that they can pounce on mice in pitch darkness by homing on their rustling movements and squeaks. Prey is carried back to a regular perch where glossy black pellets of undigested bones and fur accumulate.

○ Frequent.

○ Resident.

○ Breeding, February-July.

○ Female greyer on back.

○ Snowy owl almost pure white and very large.

○ Other owls have brown faces and a certain amount of brown on underparts.

Plumage: Orange-buff upperparts. Face and underparts white. Distinct ring around face. Length 34 cm (13½ in).
Voice: A long shriek.
Habitat: Farmland, sometimes towns. Also cliffs.
Food: Small rodents, chiefly wood mice and voles but also rats and house mice. Also birds.
Nest: In empty buildings and ruins or hollow trees, old nests of other species and cliff crevices. No nest material.
Eggs: 4-7 (3-11). White. March-April. Sometimes 2 clutches. Incubated for 33 days by female.
Young: Nidicolous. Fed by both parents. Fledge at 9-12 weeks.
In the field: Pale coloration, unstreaked underparts.

40 mm

Little Owl

Athene noctua

Little owls are found over much of Europe and Asia, except the north, and in North Africa, but have bred in Britain only since 1879. Several attempts were made to introduce this owl from the Continent but the species did not become established properly until the late 19th century. In the early 1900s the little owl spread across most of England and Wales, but has not penetrated far into Scotland.

Little owls are more active by day than most owls and they hunt mainly at dawn and dusk. They keep watch from such vantage points as telegraph poles and wires, where they can be seen bobbing up and down looking for prey. When a suitable item, such as a large insect, is seen they pounce quickly upon it. Compared with most other owls, little owls have long legs. They can run surprisingly fast and chase their prey over the ground. The flight is undulating, like a woodpecker, but the round head is unmistakable.

○ Frequent.

○ Resident.

○ Breeding, March-July.

○ Sexes similar.

○ Other owls larger.

○ In flight, woodpeckers lack rounded head.

Plumage: Upperparts brown with white spots. Underparts white with brown streaks. Juvenile paler. Length 22 cm (8½ in).
Voice: A mewing *kiew, kiew* and a repeated yelp.
Habitat: Farmland, parks.
Food: Insects, especially beetles and craneflies, small rodents. A few birds and various invertebrates.
Nest: Holes in trees, old buildings, rabbit burrows. No nest material.
Eggs: 3-5 (2-8). White. April-May. Incubated for 28 days by female.
Young: Nidicolous. Fed by both parents. Fledge at 26 days.
In the field: Small, brown owl with undulating flight.

adult

juvenile

36 mm

Tawny Owl
Strix aluco

The legendary *tu-whit tu-whoo* of the tawny owl is a mixture of several calls. A sharp *kewick* is heard mainly in the summer, when young owls also call with a *tu-whit*. The long, quavering *hoo-oo-oo* is used throughout the year, especially in autumn and winter.

The tawny owl is very nocturnal in its habits but it is sometimes seen and heard in the day, especially when it has a family to feed. Its usual method of hunting is to wait on a perch and drop on to passing prey. The favourite food is small rodents but tawny owls also catch some birds, frogs, earthworms and even fish. Many more birds are eaten in urban areas and in the countryside when voles are scarce. Contrary to popular belief, the eyesight of tawny owls is not a great deal better than human vision. Owls are efficient night hunters because they use both eyesight and hearing.

○ Common.

○ Resident.

○ Breeding, March-August.

○ Sexes similar.

○ Long-eared owl is smaller and more slender.

○ Little owl is much smaller.

○ Barn owl is pale.

Plumage: Upperparts rufous-brown with dark brown mottling. White patches on scapulars and coverts. Underparts buff with dark streaks. Juvenile paler. Length 38 cm (15 in).
Voice: *Kewick, tu-whit* and the hoot, *hoo-oo-oo*.
Habitat: Wooded farms, parks and suburbs. Also woodland.
Food: Small rodents, mainly voles. A few birds, earthworms and frogs; more if voles scarce.
Nest: Hollow trees or abandoned nests of other birds. No nest material.
Eggs: 2-4 (1-7). White. March-April. Incubated for 28 days by female.
Young: Nidicolous. Fed by both parents. Fledge at 35 days. Feeding by parents continues for another 3 months.
In the field: At rest, rounded body with large head. Rounded wings in flight.

adult

juvenile

47 mm

Nightjar
Caprimulgus europaeus

Most birds retire to roost as night falls, but the nightjar joins the owls to hunt in the dark, exploiting the wealth of night-flying insects which it scoops up with its huge, gaping mouth. A fringe of bristles protects its large eyes and increases the area of the gape for sweeping up insects.

The presence of nightjars is given away by the trilling song of the male birds. They are easiest to observe at dusk when they can be seen wheeling and jinking after insects. During the day they roost on a branch or on a nest on the ground. The camouflage pattern of their plumage breaks up the outline of the body and makes them very difficult to see.

Nightjars have become rarer over the last 50 years, mainly because many of the heaths and commons where they used to nest have been built over or planted with trees.

○ Scarce.

○ Summer visitor.

○ British Isles, May-September.

○ Breeding, May-August.

○ Males have white spots.

○ Owls have broader wings and more direct flight.

Plumage: Grey-brown with lighter and darker mottling and streaking. Male has conspicuous white spots on the primaries and the tip of the outer tail feathers. Length 27 cm (10½ in).

Voice: A far-carrying low-pitched churring which continues for several minutes.

Habitat: Mainly heaths and commons, open woods and young plantations, felled woods, downs. Also moors and dunes.

Food: Flying insects, mainly moths, beetles and craneflies.

Nest: A scrape on bare ground.

Eggs: 2 (3). Dirty white with pale brown markings. May-June and July-August. Incubated for 18 days by both sexes.

Young: Nidifugous. Fed by both parents. Fly at 18 days but fed for a further 2 weeks.

In the field: Nocturnal flight and distinctive voice.

♀

♂

32 mm

Swift
Apus apus

The swift spends more time in flight than any other bird. In fact almost its whole life is spent in the air as it usually lands only when visiting its nest. Swifts can stay airborne for such prolonged periods because they can sleep and even mate on the wing. They drink by dipping down to the water's surface. The streamlined body and slender, scythe-shaped wings are perfect for high-speed flight, although manoeuvrability is lost. Their legs are small and rather weak; all four toes point forwards and are used for clinging to vertical walls. If swifts do land on the ground they find it difficult to get back into the air.

The food of swifts is flying insects and they climb as much as 1,000 metres (3,280 ft) high to find them. They also fly many kilometres to find swarms of insects. In cold, wet weather, swifts have difficulty finding food but their young can survive for several days without being fed by letting their body temperatures drop 10°C.

○ Common.

○ Summer visitor.

○ British Isles, late April-September.

○ Breeding, May-July.

○ Sexes similar.

○ Swallows and martins have white undersides and broader wings.

Plumage: Sooty-brown with grey on the throat. Juvenile has more white on throat and narrow white border on wings. Length 17 cm (6½ in).
Voice: Screaming *swee*.
Habitat: Cities, towns and villages, especially where there are old buildings. Also cliffs.
Food: Flying insects, mainly flies.
Nest: In crevices in buildings; sometimes on cliffs. Straws and feathers picked up in the air and glued with saliva to make a cup.
Eggs: 3 (2-4). White. May-June. Incubated for 18 days by both parents.
Young: Nidicolous. Fed by both parents. Fly at 35-36 days depending on weather.
In the field: Uniform dark colour, streamlined shape with swept-back wings and slightly forked tail. Noisy wheeling groups during breeding season.

juvenile

adult

25 mm

Kingfisher
Alcedo atthis

Despite its brilliant coloration, the kingfisher is often overlooked completely or seen only as a brilliant blue flash streaking over the water. It is shy, but a careful observer may be lucky enough to see a kingfisher hunting. It keeps watch from a perch, or by hovering, and plunges into the water to grasp a small fish. Once the prey is caught the kingfisher starts to flap its wings, bringing it to the surface and rising into the air without a check.

Kingfishers nest in burrows which are excavated in banks, sometimes quite far from water. They fly at the bank to dislodge soil with the bill until the hole is large enough for them to land and continue the excavation. The nest becomes extremely foul so that the adults have to wash after visiting. The growing feathers of the nestlings are protected in waxy sheaths until they are ready to leave the nest.

○ Frequent.

○ Resident.

○ Breeding, April-August.

○ Female has orange patch on bill.

Plumage: Upperparts brilliant blue, shot with green. Underparts chestnut. Throat white. Chestnut and white patches behind eye. Juveniles duller. Length 17 cm (6½ in).

Voice: A shrill call and a trilling song.

Habitat: Any fresh water, including built-up areas. Also estuaries and rocky coasts in winter.

Food: Mainly small fish. Also water insects, snails and amphibians.

Nest: A tunnel up to 1 metre (39 in) long, dug by both sexes.

Eggs: 6-7 (4-10). White. April-May. 2 clutches. Incubated for 20 days by both parents.

Young: Nidicolous. Fed by both parents. Fly at 25 days but fed for longer period.

In the field: Brilliant blue, squat body, long bill and rapid wingbeats.

adult

juvenile

⌐ 23 mm

Hoopoe
Upupa epops

The hoopoe is one of the most spectacular and easily recognized visitors to this country, for there is no mistaking the broad black and white wings and the bouncing jinking flight. The fan-shaped, black-tipped crest is opened at intervals both on the ground and in flight, and especially on landing. The distinctive call has given the bird both its English and scientific names. Once spotted, its habit of feeding on open ground, such as lawns and paths, makes the hoopoe an easy bird to observe.

The hoopoe is a bird of the Mediterranean regions, although it nests as far north as Sweden. Most hoopoes seen in Britain have flown too far on migration and have overshot their usual summer homes. They are most common on the south coast of England, but a few reach northern Scotland and Shetland. Hoopoes can usually be seen from March to May. On rare occasions, a pair of hoopoes may stay to nest in one of the southern counties.

○ Rare.

○ Summer visitor.

○ British Isles, mainly March-May.

○ Does not nest in the British Isles.

○ Sexes similar.

○ Jay has pale blue on wings, slight crest, short bill and black 'moustache'.

○ Great and lesser woodpeckers have no pink plumage but have red on head. No crest, short bill.

Plumage: Pink-brown body and head with black-tipped crest. The broad, rounded wings, and tail, are striped with black and white. Juvenile similar to adults. Length 28 cm (11 in).

Voice: A soft, far-carrying *hoop-hoop-hoop*.

Habitat: Large gardens and parks. Also open woods.

Food: Mainly insect larvae, but also adult insects and other invertebrates.

Nest: In hollow trees, piles of stones and other crevices. Usually no lining but food remains and accumulation of droppings.

Eggs: 5-8. Dirty white or yellowish. May-June. Incubated for 18 days by female who is fed by male.

Young: Nidicolous. Fed by both parents. Fly in 3-4 weeks.

In the field: Broad black and white wings. Distinctive crest and long, curved bill.

adult

adult

26 mm

Wryneck

Jynx torquilla

The name wryneck comes from the bird's habit of twisting its neck when threatening and during courtship. An interesting bird, it is particularly disappointing that it is becoming rare. It has almost ceased breeding in south-east England but wrynecks from Scandinavia have started to nest in northern Scotland.

The wryneck shares several characteristics with its woodpecker relatives. One toe is turned back to help cling to tree trunks and the tail feathers are sometimes used as a prop. The tongue is long and is used for picking up insects. However, the wryneck cannot chisel into wood to find insects or to make its own nest hole. It has to rely on natural holes or nestboxes and picks insects from crevices in the bark or off the ground.

When the wryneck is disturbed on the nest, its neck weaves from side to side, the tongue flicks in and out and a hissing sound completes the imitation of an angry snake.

○ Rare.

○ Summer visitor.

○ British Isles, March-October.

○ Breeding, May-July.

○ Sexes similar.

○ Kestrel has similar call.

○ Woodpeckers more conspicuous.

○ Treecreeper smaller, pale underneath.

Plumage: Grey-brown, mottled and streaked above and barred below. There are dark lines down the back and through the eyes. The underparts and wings appear darker than the back and tail. Juvenile paler. Length 17 cm (6½ in).

Voice: Shrill *kee-kee-kee.*

Habitat: Parks, gardens and orchards, commons. Also woodland.

Food: Insects, mainly ants.

Nest: Hole in a tree or wall. No nest material.

Eggs: 7-10 (5-12). White. May-June. Incubated for 12 days by both parents.

Young: Nidicolous. Fed by both parents. Fly at 20 days.

In the field: Call. Slender, grey form.

21 mm

Green Woodpecker
Picus viridis

The green woodpecker's nickname is 'yaffle' which describes the clear laughing call that often reveals its presence. As well as looking for insects on the trunks and branches of trees, it feeds on the ground. A favourite food is ants, and green woodpeckers are often seen in lawns and grasslands which have been cropped short by sheep or rabbits. When disturbed, they fly back to the trees with the woodpeckers' characteristic undulating flight – flapping up for three or four beats then gliding down with wings closed. Unlike the other smaller woodpeckers, the green woodpecker very rarely 'drums' by rapping the tree with its bill.

Woodpeckers extract insects from the bark of trees by chiselling holes in the wood with their strong, pointed bills. The insect is then removed with the tongue, which in the case of the green woodpecker is an incredible 15 cm (6 in) long. The woodpecker grips the tree trunk with its strong toes, obtaining extra support from its stiff tail feathers.

○ Frequent.

○ Resident.

○ Breeding, February-June.

○ Sexes differ in moustachial stripe.

○ Hoopoe has black and white wings and crest.

○ Great and lesser spotted woodpeckers are black and white.

○ Jay is pinkish-brown with light blue on wings.

Plumage: Head and body green, darker above. Rump yellow-green. Face black and crown a very distinct red. Male has red moustachial stripe with black border; female's is all black. Juvenile is streaked and spotted. Length 32 cm (12½ in).
Voice: A far-carrying laugh.
Habitat: Parks and gardens with trees and lawns. Also open woodland and heaths with trees.
Food: Mainly wood-boring insects and ants, and occasionally fruits and seeds.
Nest: An unlined hollow excavated in a tree trunk. Made by both sexes.
Eggs: 5-7 (4-9). White, sometimes stained brown by wood. April-May. Incubated for 18 days by both sexes.
Young: Nidicolous. Fed by both parents. Fly at 18-21 days.
In the field: Green plumage with red crown and yellow rump.

juvenile

adult

32 mm

Woodlark
Lullula arborea

LARKS
Alaudidae

The woodlark has become scarce over the last century and, since it is so similar to the familiar skylark, a special effort has to be made to spot it. The best way of finding the woodlark is to listen out for its song, which is not only easy to detect but also distinct from the skylark's. Whereas the skylark flutters up vertically, singing as it rises and hovers for minutes on end, the woodlark flies from one tree or bush to another in a slow circling path. The rich, musical song comprises a brief series of descending phrases, of variable form. A common series might be written as *ulla-ulla-ulla* – hence the scientific name.

The decline of the woodlark is probably due to cold, wet springs and summers rather than to severe winters. It lays early and is vulnerable to late snows. The young leave the nest before they can fly and hide nearby.

○ Scarce.

○ Resident.

○ Breeding, March-July.

○ Sexes similar.

○ Skylark has distinctive song, white on sides of tail and on trailing edges of wings, shorter eyestripes, no black patch on wing.

○ Pipits lack crest, have different song.

Plumage: Upperparts brown with dark streaking. Underparts buffish-white with spots and streaks on breast. White eye-stripes reach around neck. Tail brown in the centre, black outside with white at the corners. Black mark on 'wrist'. Length 15 cm (6 in).

Voice: Series of about 10 descending phrases.

Habitat: Dry country. Farms with scattered trees, heaths and commons.

Food: Mainly insects but many seeds in autumn.

Nest: Cup of woven grasses with finer lining on ground. Built by both sexes.

Eggs: 3-4 (1-6). Dirty white with fine brown spots. March-July. 2, sometimes 3 clutches. Incubated for 14 days by female.

Young: Nidicolous. Fed by both parents. Fledge at 12 days but leave nest earlier.

In the field: Song. Slight crest like other larks. White eyestripes and black mark on wings.

adult

juvenile

22 mm

Sand Martin
Riparia riparia

This is the first of the four aerial insect-eaters to return from winter quarters in Africa. The appearance of sand martins flying over lakes and rivers is one of the signs of spring. They soon make their way to banks and cliffs where they either excavate new burrows, up to a metre (39 in) or more long, or re-occupy old ones. The increase in sand and gravel quarrying has provided sand martins with many new nesting places, but continuing extraction or natural erosion, as in river banks, has led to the destruction of colonies. Local populations may suffer if other sites are not available.

After nesting, sand martins gather in huge roosts, usually in reedbeds, before migrating. One roost is known to harbour two million birds. The juveniles leave the nesting area first. They wander around the country and may travel 100 kilometres (60 miles) or more to new feeding grounds and roosts. Eventually all the sand martins head south, through western France and Spain to West Africa.

○ Common.

○ Summer visitor.

○ British Isles, March-September.

○ Breeding, May-August.

○ Sexes similar.

○ Swift uniformly dark.

○ Swallow has deeply forked tail.

○ House martin has white rump.

Plumage: Upperparts dark brown. Underparts white with brown band across breast. Juvenile similar with buff throat. Length 13 cm (5 in).
Voice: Harsh twittering.
Habitat: Open country near water, where there are suitable nesting places – mainly river banks and gravel pits, also coastal cliffs and cuttings.
Food: Flying insects, mainly flies and aphids.
Nest: Burrow in sand or earth with chamber lined with straw and feathers. Built by both sexes.
Eggs: 4-5 (3-7). White. May-July. 2 clutches. Incubated by both sexes for 14 days.
Young: Nidicolous. Fed by both parents. Fly at 22 days.
In the field: Brown upperparts, slightly forked tail. Fluttering flight.

juvenile

adult

18 mm

Swallow
Hirundo rustica

British swallows spend the winter in southern Africa and take one month to fly back to Britain in the spring. They spread northwards through Europe as the weather gets warmer, halting if there is a cold spell or speeding on if the weather is fine. Many die in the long crossing of the Sahara. On their arrival, the swallows haunt wet meadows and marshes before seeking out their old nesting sites on houses, barns and sheds. In the days before human habitations provided a convenient place for the nest of mud and grass, swallows nested on cliffs, in caves and on trees. A few still do today. Old buildings with rafters and other irregularities to form a foundation are the preferred nest sites.

Although not such speedy fliers as swifts, the swallows' broad wings give them superior manoeuvrability for chasing flying insects. During the summer they can be seen flying a few centimetres above the ground as they search for food.

○ Common.

○ Summer visitor.

○ British Isles, March/April-September/October (sometimes November).

○ Breeding, April-July.

○ Female duller with shorter tail streamers.

○ Swift is uniformly dark.

○ House martin has white rump.

Plumage: Head and underparts blue-black, with chestnut on throat and forehead. Underparts white or pale buff. Row of white flecks on tail. Female has shorter tail streamers and has more brown on throat. Juvenile has short tail streamers and is brown rather than blue. Length 18 cm (7 in).
Voice: A quiet twittering.
Habitat: Open country, including parks. Often over water and marshes. Buildings nearly always necessary for nesting.
Food: Flying insects, mainly flies.
Nest: A cup of mud mixed with grass and hair, fixed to buildings. Built by both sexes.
Eggs: 4-5 (3-8). White with fine brown specks. May-June. 2-3 clutches. Incubated for 14-15 days by female, rarely male.
Young: Nidicolous. Fed by both parents. Fly at 21 days.
In the field: Dark above, white below and long tail streamers. Often flies very low.

20 mm

House Martin
Delichon urbica

The habits of the house martin are similar to those of the swallows but there are important differences. The two birds are alike in migrating to Africa, feeding on flying insects and nesting on buildings. However, house martins return a week or so later than swallows. They nest on the outside of buildings and adapt to the smooth exteriors of modern houses better. Where air pollution has been controlled by Smokeless Zones, so that flying insects can thrive, house martins have moved into city centres. On the other hand, they still nest regularly on cliffs.

House martins are sociable birds. Like swallows, they perch in flocks on telephone wires and small groups nest together under eaves, with the nests sometimes touching. Nest boxes often attract martins to a house and other pairs will join them and build natural nests. The young of one brood may help to feed the second brood and the whole family roosts in the nest.

○ Common.

○ Summer visitor.

○ British Isles,
April/May-August/October.

○ Breeding, May-August.

○ Sexes similar.

○ Swift is uniformly dark.

○ Swallow lacks white rump and has long tail streamers.

○ Sand martin is brown instead of blue-black.

Plumage: Head and upperparts blue-black with white rump. Underparts white; underside of wing black. Juvenile brown rather than black. Length 13 cm (5 in).
Voice: Soft twittering.
Habitat: Open country and towns. Also cliff regions.
Food: Flying insects, mainly flies.
Nest: Cup of mud pellets under eaves. Built by both sexes.
Eggs: 4-5 (2-6). White. May-June. 2 clutches. Incubated by both sexes for 14 days.
Young: Nidicolous. Fed by both parents. Fly at 21 days.
In the field: Dark above, white below and on rump.

106

19 mm

Pied Wagtail
Motacilla alba

The natural home of the pied wagtail is along streams and rivers where it can feed among shingle banks and boulders or in neighbouring meadows. Nowadays, it has become closely associated with human habitations. Pied wagtails are a common sight around farms and in parks and gardens. In winter, they may roost in factories and greenhouses.

Watching wagtails as they hunt insects on a lawn is a pleasant occupation. They walk or run briskly with heads nodding to and fro and tails wagging. Every now and then, one rushes forward or flies up to seize an insect. When it stops moving, the tail continues to wag. The nodding head helps the bird to spot small insects by moving the insect's image across the sensitive structures at the back of its eye. The long wagging tail may be to help maintain balance and to steer the bird in its sudden rushes and changes of direction.

- Common.
- Resident.
- Breeding, April-August.
- Female greyer with less black.
- Magpie very much larger.
- Grey and yellow wagtails have yellow underparts.

Plumage: Male's summer plumage has black upperparts, throat and breast. Forehead, sides of face, belly, outer tail feathers and wing bars are white. In winter the throat is white and the back is greyer. The female is greyer with less black on head and breast. Juvenile brownish rather than black. Continental race, called the white wagtail, occurs as a migrant. The male has a grey back and less black on the breast. Length 18 cm (7 in).

Voice: Sharp *tissick* and a twittering song.

Habitat: Farms, towns and gardens.

Food: Small insects, mainly flies.

Nest: Untidy cup of leaves and twigs, lined with feathers and hair, in hole in wall, bank or tree. Built by female.

Eggs: 5-6 (3-7). Dirty white with grey or brown spots. April-July. 2-3 clutches. Incubated for 14 days, mainly by female.

Young: Nidicolous. Fed by both parents. Fly at 15 days.

In the field: Long tail, black and white plumage.

adult

juvenile

21 mm

Waxwing
Bombycilla garrulus

The home of the strikingly coloured waxwing is the coniferous forest of northern Scandinavia, Russia and Siberia. A few waxwings wander south each winter but, at intervals of about ten years, there is an invasion of central and southern Europe, including the British Isles. Such an irregular migration is called an irruption. The exact cause is not fully understood but it is probably due to a failure of the rowan berry crop, the waxwings' favourite food. If this comes at a time when waxwings are very numerous, they must disperse in search of alternative food.

When waxwings arrive in Britain they search for rowans but they also eat the berries of yew, holly and elder, among others. Waxwings often come into towns where they are attracted to cotoneaster and pyracantha, and come to birdtables to feed on bread and seeds. They are sometimes very tame and easy to approach, when the red and yellow 'waxy' blobs on wings and tail can be seen.

○ Scarce.

○ Winter visitor.

○ British Isles, October-March.

○ Does not nest in the British Isles.

○ Sexes almost similar.

Plumage: Head, including crest, neck and breast pinkish brown with black line through eyes and under chin. Rest of body greyish brown. Primaries black with yellow line, secondaries grey with red waxy blobs. Tail grey and black with yellow waxy tips. Undertail coverts chestnut. Female greyish on body and generally less bright. Juvenile lacks black throat and yellow wing and is duller. Length 18 cm (7 in).

Voice: A high *sirr*.

Habitat: Gardens and farms with hedgerows and trees. Also woodland.

Food: Insects and berries in summer. Berries and seeds in winter.

Nest: A cup of twigs and lichen built by the female.

Eggs: 4-6. Grey-blue with many black spots. Incubated for 14 days by the female.

Young: Nidicolous. Fed by both parents. Fly at 14 days.

In the field: Chestnut head and crest, yellow tip of tail.

♂

24 mm

Wren
Troglodytes troglodytes

Although often believed to be the smallest British bird, the wren is in fact larger than the goldcrest. Nevertheless people have always been impressed by its small size. Folk tales tell how the wren became King of the Birds by beating the eagle with subterfuge, and there used to be an annual wren hunt in many parts of the country, a ritual dating back thousands of years.

Wrens are one of the most common nesting birds in Britain and their cheery song can be heard almost everywhere. They are hard hit by severe winters and there is little one can do to help them as they rarely come to birdtables, although they may sometimes take odd scraps from the ground. However, their numbers recover in a few years. On cold winter nights, wrens huddle together in roosts to keep warm. In spring, male wrens build several nests in their territories but only one is eventually lined with feathers and has eggs laid in it. Sometimes a male has more than one mate.

○ Common.

○ Resident.

○ Breeding, March–August.

○ Sexes similar.

○ Goldcrest has yellow and black on crown.

○ Dunnock is similarly secretive but larger and grey underneath.

Plumage: Brown, more russet above and buff below, with distinct barring on flanks, wings and tail. Pale eyestripe. Juvenile mottled underneath and barring fainter. Length 10 cm (4 in).
Voice: Clicking *tick-tick-tick* and loud, rambling and trilling song.
Habitat: Farmland and gardens. Also woods, moors and seacliffs.
Food: Insects, especially caterpillars.
Nest: A hollow ball of dead leaves and moss in a bush or crevice. Built by male, lined with feathers by female.
Eggs: 5-6 (3-7). White with red-brown spots. April-July. 2 clutches. Incubated for 15 days by female.
Young: Nidicolous. Fed by both parents. Fly at 16 days.
In the field: Song. Small size and turned-up tail. Whirring flight.

17 mm

Dunnock
Prunella modularis

This bird used to be called the hedge sparrow but, because it is not a true sparrow, the old country name of dunnock is preferred. The slender bill and grey underparts immediately distinguish it from the true sparrows. It likes low cover where it can skulk quietly and these conditions are provided by hedgerows and the rank growth of derelict ground. Dunnocks usually keep near the ground and feed on food spilled from birdtables, rather than visiting the tables themselves.

The retiring habits and dull plumage of the dunnock have led to its being ignored by bird watchers. Surprisingly little is known about the dunnock's habits but it can never be overlooked completely because of its song. This is a rambling trill rather similar to the song of the wren, and can be heard for most of the year. The dull appearance of the bird is redeemed by the beauty of its sky-blue eggs.

○ Common.

○ Resident.

○ Breeding, April-August.

○ Sexes similar.

○ Sparrows have stouter bills and bold markings on head.

Plumage: Dark brown on back and wings with streaks. Head and underparts grey or greyish-brown. Length 15 cm (6 in).
Voice: Shrill *seep* and a thin shrill warbling song.
Habitat: Farmland with hedges, gardens and parks. Also moors with cover and woods.
Food: Insects, spiders and worms in summer. Seeds of weeds in winter.
Nest: Cup of twigs and leaves lined with moss and hair. Built by female.
Eggs: 4-5 (3-6). Blue, sometimes with red spots. April-July. 2-3 clutches. Incubated for 12 days by female.
Young: Nidicolous. Fed by both parents. Fly at 12 days.
In the field: Song. Thin bill. Grey underparts.

20 mm

Robin
Erithacus rubecula

The election of the robin as the British National Bird is due to its tameness. Strangely, robins are shy woodland dwellers on the Continent and are not easily seen. Even in Britain, robins have not always been popular because their song was sometimes supposed to tell of approaching bad weather. Their delightful habit of feeding close by gardeners is a relic from the days when robins followed large forest animals, picking up small insects exposed as the leaf litter was turned by their feet.

Robins are well known for their aggression towards each other in the defence of their territories. Female robins also hold territories and sing to advertise them in early winter but pairs form and share territories in the New Year. Towards the end of summer adult robins appear to vanish. It was once believed that they had been killed by their offspring. In reality, the adults moult at this time and become very quiet and shy.

○ Common.

○ Resident.

○ Breeding, March-August.

○ Sexes similar.

○ Bullfinch more pink and has black cap and white rump.

Plumage: Brown above with orange-red forehead, throat and breast, with grey border. Belly white. Juvenile lacks red and has pale spots. Length 14 cm (5½ in).
Voice: Harsh *tick-tick*. Sweet, liquid warbling song.
Habitat: Farmland, parks and gardens. Also woodland.
Food: Mainly insects, with worms and some seeds and berries.
Nest: Cup of dead leaves, lined with moss. Often in hollows, old tins, sheds etc. Built by female.
Eggs: 5-6 (3-9). White with reddish spots. April-July. 2 or 3 clutches. Incubated for 14 days by female.
Young: Nidicolous. Fed by both parents. Fly at 14 days.
In the field: Red breast.

juvenile

adult

20 mm

Black Redstart
Phoenicurus ochruros

After reading about birds which are declining in numbers, it is always heartening to learn of one which is spreading. The black redstart is a visitor to Britain which has stayed to breed. Its original nesting places were on the rocky slopes of mountainous areas but a few have adapted to life in towns, where docks, power stations, gas works and derelict sites provide man-made equivalents to cliffs and screes. Favourite nesting places are ledges and cavities, both inside and outside buildings.

After one or two false starts, black redstarts bred regularly in England during the 1920s, when they nested first on Sussex cliffs and then in Cornwall. In 1926 some birds moved into London and took up residence in a derelict exhibition site. The war provided suitable nesting places in the form of bombed sites and the black redstart has since spread to other urban and coastal areas. On average, some 30 pairs nest each year.

○ Rare.

○ Summer and winter visitor.

○ British Isles, March-November.

○ Breeding, April-July.

○ Male grey-black; female brown.

○ Redstart has rufous underparts; male has distinct black mask.

Plumage: Male is grey on the back and on the crown. The tail is chestnut with black in the centre. White patch on wing. In winter the forehead, sides of head, throat and breast are black. In summer this area is grey. Females and juveniles are overall greyish-brown except for the chestnut and black tail. Length 14 cm (5½ in).

Voice: A warble that ends in a rattle like ball bearings shaken together.

Habitat: Industrial and derelict ground in towns. Also sea cliffs.

Food: Insects, especially small beetles, ants, flies and caterpillars. Some berries.

Nest: Cup of grasses and moss lined with feathers in a ledge or crevice. Built by female.

Eggs: 4-6. White. April-June. 2-3 clutches. Incubated for 12 days by female.

Young: Nidicolous. Fed by both parents. Fly at 17 days.

In the field: Grey underparts, red tail, white on wing.

♂

♀

19 mm

Redstart
Phoenicurus phoenicurus

Redstart means 'red tail'. It is a summer visitor, arriving in Europe in April or May after a winter spent, like so many small insect-eating birds, in the countries lying south of the Sahara. Though redstarts can easily be overlooked by the casual observer their red tails make them easily recognizable. They often perch in the open on trees and fences and move about restlessly in search of insects found among the foliage or caught in the air. During the spring the male makes himself extra conspicuous with his jingling song which is often delivered in flight. At rest the red tail is constantly flicked up and down.

Nesting gets under way soon after the redstarts have returned in spring. This haste is necessary so that the chicks may hatch when there is an abundance of the caterpillars and flying insects on which they are fed. The caterpillars will not be easy to find a few weeks later.

○ Frequent.

○ Summer visitor.

○ British Isles, April-October.

○ Breeding, April-July.

○ Males have black on head.

○ Robin lacks red tail and black head.

○ Black redstart lacks white crown and red underparts.

Plumage: Male has grey upperparts with some white on the crown. Face and throat are black, underparts and tail orange-red. Female less colourful and brownish above, lacking the black on the head. Juvenile similar to female. Length 14 cm (5½ in).

Voice: Short song, rather like a robin's, but ending with a jingle.

Habitat: Parks and gardens, farms with old hedges or drystone walls. Also moors and woodland.

Food: Insects, especially caterpillars and flies. A few spiders and worms.

Nest: Grasses and moss, lined with feathers in a hollow tree, cavity in a wall or nest box. Built by female.

Eggs: 6 (5-7). Pale blue. April-June. 2 clutches. Incubated for 14 days by female.

Young: Nidicolous. Fed by both parents. Fly at 14 days.

In the field: Red tail and underparts. Robin-like behaviour.

19 mm

Blackbird
Turdus merula

The blackbird is one of the most common birds in Britain. Essentially a woodland bird, it has made full use of gardens and is now more common in suburbia than anywhere else. It draws attention to itself by its mellow, fluting song and by its alarm calls. There is the metallic *chook-chook* when the blackbird is mildly alarmed, perhaps by a prowling cat, and the shrieking rattle when it is surprised and flies off to safety.

Part of the blackbird's success is due to its varied diet. It comes regularly to birdtables; it eats insects and is fond of fruit. It is a common sight to see a blackbird hop across the lawn, stop to 'eye' the ground and then plunge forward to pull out a worm.

The black male and brown female are easily recognized and young males in their first winter have brown bills. Juveniles have speckled breasts and are sometimes mistakenly thought to be a cross between a blackbird and a thrush.

○ Common.

○ Resident.

○ Breeding, February-July.

○ Male black, female brown.

○ Ring ouzel has white bib.

Plumage: Male is black except for the yellow beak and yellow eye-ring. Female is dark brown with some mottling underneath. Juveniles are lighter with more mottling. There is sometimes a greater or lesser amount of white. Length 25 cm (10 in).

Voice: Rattling alarm calls. Song is a mellow, repeated warble.

Habitat: Gardens, parkland, farmland. Also woods, moors and hills.

Food: Earthworms, insects, occasional frog or shrew. Fruit and seeds.

Nest: A cup of grasses and moss, lined with mud and a layer of fine grasses. Built by female.

Eggs: 4-5 (3-9). Bluish-green sometimes with brown markings. April-July. 2-3 clutches. Incubated for 13 days by female.

Young: Nidicolous. Fed by both parents. Fly at 13 days.

In the field: Black male, brown female.

♂

♀

29 mm

Fieldfare
Turdus pilaris

THRUSHES
Turdidae

Fieldfares arrive in Britain from Scandinavia every winter and their loose flocks make a fine sight on a clear, frosty day, either as they fly over with a jaunty, flicking action or as they quarter the fields. These flocks are nomadic, descending on the haws growing in a hedge, or the berries in a holly tree, and stripping the crop before moving on.

Since 1967 an increasing number of fieldfares have stayed in Britain to nest instead of returning to Scandinavia. This is part of a general spread of the fieldfare through Europe. Most nesting has taken place in Scotland but a few pairs have bred in northern England. At the moment, breeding pairs are very scattered, but this may change if larger numbers nest here. In Scandinavia, fieldfares nest in groups and several pairs sometimes nest in one tree. They are very aggressive and attack people who come too close to the nests by swooping at them and screaming noisily.

○ Common.

○ Winter visitor (and resident).

○ British Isles, September-May.

○ Breeding, April-July.

○ Sexes similar.

○ No other thrushes have grey head and rump.

Plumage: Brown back and wings. Head, nape and rump slate grey. Tail black. Underparts brown to white with black streaks. White under wing. Length 25 cm (10 in).
Voice: Harsh *chack-chack-chack*. Song is a rather blackbird-like warbling and whistling.
Habitat: Farms and gardens. Nests in woods and on moors.
Food: Fruit and seeds. Insects, worms and other invertebrates.
Nest: Like a blackbird's, made of grasses and mud with a grass lining.
Eggs: 5-6 (3-8). Greenish-blue, sometimes with brown markings. April-July. Sometimes 2 clutches. Incubated for 14 days by female.
Young: Nidicolous. Fed by both parents. Fly at 14 days.
In the field: Grey head and rump. White undersides of wings. Long black tail.

29 mm

Song Thrush
Turdus philomelos

If it is difficult to remember the difference between the songs of the blackbird and song thrush, remember Robert Browning's lines: 'That's the wise thrush; he sings each song twice over, lest you should think he never could recapture the first fine careless rapture.' Many of the phrases of the song thrush's song are repeated two or more times and are more clearly and distinctly enunciated than a blackbird's.

Song thrushes are not as common as blackbirds and they are not as sociable. Groups of blackbirds are a common sight in the winter but song thrushes remain alone or in pairs.

No other common bird has learnt the trick of smashing snails to get at the soft bodies within. The thrush holds the snail by the rim of the shell and hammers it repeatedly against a stone or against a concrete path in a garden. One stone may be used many times and these 'thrushes' anvils' become surrounded by fragments of shells.

○ Common.

○ Resident.

○ Breeding, March-July.

○ Sexes similar.

○ Redwing has red flanks.

○ Mistle thrush has larger spots.

○ Fieldfare has grey head and rump.

Plumage: Rich brown above, underparts pale buff with many small dark spots. Yellow-brown under the wings. Length 23 cm (9 in).

Voice: Alarm calls rather like blackbird's. Song has varied, very clear phrases, often repeated.

Habitat: Gardens, parks and farms. Woods.

Food: Mainly earthworms, slugs and snails. Also insects, fruit and seeds.

Nest: Grasses, leaves and twigs lined with mud or dung. Built by female.

Eggs: 4-5 (3-6). Greenish-blue with few brown spots. February-June. 2-3 clutches. Incubated for 14 days by female.

Young: Nidicolous. Fed by both parents. Fly at 14 days.

In the field: Speckled breast.

28 mm

Redwing
Turdus iliacus

Like the fieldfare, the redwing is a native of Scandinavia and visits Britain in winter where it is now becoming established as a breeding bird. The arrival of redwings is affected by the weather. If there is high pressure west of Norway, winds bring the birds from Scandinavia to the British Isles. Often the first sign of their presence is a thin, but far-carrying *see-ee*, often heard at night as the flocks migrate in. Sometimes huge numbers arrive overnight, when an anticyclone over Scandinavia causes easterly winds over the North Sea. Redwings seem to prefer fields, and come into gardens mainly in bad weather. Their diet consists of more animal food than fieldfares but they gather to strip the fruit from hedges and trees. At night, they roost in dense bushes.

Redwings have bred in Scotland since 1925, rarely at first but regularly in the last 10-15 years. There are now probably 300 breeding pairs in Scotland, mostly in the Highlands.

○ Common.

○ Winter visitor (and resident).

○ British Isles, September-April.

○ Breeding, April-August.

○ Sexes similar.

○ No other thrushes have cream eye stripe and red flanks.

Plumage: Brown above and buff with dark streaks below. Chestnut on flanks and under wing. Broad cream stripe above eye. Length 20 cm (8 in).

Voice: Thin *see-ee* in flight. Communal *chuck-chuck* by flock on ground. Song is about half a dozen fluting notes followed by a weak jingle.

Habitat: Farmlands and gardens. Nests in woods.

Food: Worms, slugs and snails, insects. Berries.

Nest: Grasses and twigs, lined with mud and fine grass. Built by female.

Eggs: 5-6 (2-7). Pale green with fine brown markings. May-July. 2 clutches. Incubated for 13 days by both partners.

Young: Nidicolous. Fed by both parents. Fly at 13 days.

In the field: Red flanks and under wings. White stripe above eye.

26 mm

Mistle Thrush
Turdus viscivorus

The mistle or missel thrush is well named. Like other thrushes it eats plenty of fruit but no other is so attracted to the sticky berries of mistletoe. Mistletoe is a parasitic plant which grows on the branches of trees, sending its roots deep into their tissues to extract minerals and water. When a bird tries to eat a mistletoe berry the sticky flesh gums up its bill and it has to wipe it off against a branch. If the seed is left in the flesh it germinates and penetrates the bark.

A good place to see mistle thrushes is on large lawns and playing fields since they boldly come out to feed some distance from cover. They will attack crows, hawks and even people in defence of their nests. They have also earned the name 'storm-cock' because they start to sing early in spring and can be heard in full voice while clinging to bare branches lashed by wind and rain.

○ Common.

○ Resident.

○ Breeding, January-June.

○ Sexes similar.

○ Song thrush has smaller spots and no grey on back or white on tail.

○ Fieldfare has grey head and rump.

○ Redwing has red flanks.

Plumage: Brown, tinged with grey above. White tip to outer tail feathers. Buffish-white with large spots underneath. White underwing. Juveniles have whitish heads. Length 27 cm (10½ in).
Voice: Tuck-tuck notes. Short song is loud, rather like a blackbird, and tends to be repeated.
Habitat: Gardens. Farms in winter. Also woodland.
Food: Fruits and small animals including worms and insects.
Nest: Grasses, roots and earth lined with grasses. Built by female.
Eggs: 4 (3-6). Cream to bluish with brown spots. February to June. Incubated for 13 days by female.
Young: Nidicolous. Fed by both parents. Fly at 14 days.
In the field: Large thrush, greyish above with big spots on breast.

31 mm

Sedge Warbler
Acrocephalus schoenobaenus

Warblers are tiny birds, weighing around 10 grammes (⅓ oz), yet they are amazing long-distance travellers, flying to Africa to spend the winter in the tropical countries to the south of the Sahara. The 4,000-kilometre (2,500-mile) journey is usually accomplished in several stages, although sometimes they manage it non-stop if conditions are favourable. To accomplish such long journeys, birds must carry large amounts of fat as fuel. The sedge warbler feeds intensively before its journey and its weight can double. The bird then becomes plump and has difficulty in taking off.

Once back in Europe, sedge warblers can be readily located by their song and are one of the easiest warblers to identify by sight. Although most closely associated with damp places at the edges of lakes and rivers where they live among osiers, reeds and rank vegetation, sedge warblers are also found in hedgerows and among crops.

- ◯ Frequent.
- ◯ Summer visitor.
- ◯ British Isles, March-September.
- ◯ Breeding, April-July.
- ◯ Sexes similar.
- ◯ Reed warbler lacks streaking and eyestripe.

Plumage: Brown upperparts, with more tawny rump. The crown is heavily streaked with dark brown, the back less so. The closed wings appear streaked. Underparts creamy-white. Bold creamy eye-stripe. Juvenile more yellowish with faint spots on breast. Length 13 cm (5 in).

Voice: Varied succession of loud, twittering notes, often repeated.

Habitat: Mainly marshy areas but also farmland.

Food: Insects, especially flies and bugs.

Nest: A cup of grass and moss, lined with hair or grassheads, built near the ground by female.

Eggs: 5-6 (3-7). Dense yellow speckling. May-June. 2 or 3 clutches. Incubated for 14 days by female.

Young: Nidicolous. Fed by both parents. Fly at 14 days.

In the field: Song. Streaked plumage with plain rump and conspicuous eyestripe.

18 mm

Reed Warbler
Acrocephalus scirpaceus

The reed warbler is more restricted to wet places than the sedge warbler, although the two often live side by side in reedbeds. Occasionally the reed warbler belies its name and inhabits dense growths of willowherb, nettles and meadowsweet; sometimes it may come into gardens and parks.

Although warblers usually skulk in cover and are difficult to see, their noisy, distinctive song gives them away. Reed warblers are particularly easy to find once a suitable reedbed has been located, and they can often be seen flitting between the stems.

The territorial behaviour of birds was first studied by an amateur ornithologist, Eliot Howard, who made observations on reed warblers. The males return from Africa first and establish themselves in reedbeds where they sing to defend the boundaries of their territory. The females arrive later and the nest is built in the territory, although both sexes go farther afield to gather food.

○ Frequent.

○ Summer visitor.

○ British Isles, April-October.

○ Breeding, April-July.

○ Sexes similar.

○ Sedge warbler has streaked upperparts and conspicuous eyestripe.

Plumage: Plain brown above, more rufous on the rump, with pale buff underparts and white throat. Length 13 cm (5 in).
Voice: A continuous, slow chatter of harsh, distinct notes.
Habitat: Reed beds and other wet areas, including surrounds of gravel pits. Sometimes gardens and parks.
Food: Insects, mainly flies and various aquatic insects.
Nest: A deep cup of grasses, lined with finer grass, reed flowers etc., and fixed to vertical reed or other stems. Built by female.
Eggs: 4 (3-5). Very pale green with dark green markings. May-July. 1 or 2 clutches. Incubated for 11 days, mainly by female. Often parasitized by cuckoos.
Young: Nidicolous. Fed by both parents. Fly at 17 days but may leave the nest much earlier.
In the field: Song. Nondescript brown bird in reeds.

18 mm

Whitethroat/Lesser Whitethroat
Sylvia communis/Sylvia curruca

At one time the whitethroat was the most abundant warbler in a countryside of fields and lanes bordered with hedges. It was also found in rough patches and overgrown gardens, advertising its presence with a babbling song given by the male during a flight of 15 metres (16 yards) before parachuting back to cover. Then, in 1969, more than three-quarters of our whitethroats failed to return from Africa and their numbers have not recovered since. A long period of drought had hit the countries on the south side of the Sahara. This left the whitethroats short of food for the return migration and many of them perished.

The lesser whitethroat *(Sylvia curruca)* can easily be confused with the whitethroat at first sight but their songs are different. It is more likely to be seen in taller, denser hedges and gardens with trees, and delivers its song from cover rather than during a song-flight.

Whitethroat

Lesser whitethroat

○ Frequent.

○ Summer visitor.

○ British Isles, March-October.

○ Breeding, April-July.

○ Male has grey cap.

○ Garden warbler lacks grey cap of male and white outer tail feathers.

Plumage: Upperparts brown, more rufous on wings. Underparts buff, with white throat. Male has grey head and pinkish tinge to breast. Lesser whitethroat generally greyer and has dark 'mask' over eyes. Length 14 cm (5½ in).

Voice: A babbling warble. Lesser whitethroat has rattle on one note.

Habitat: Farmland and gardens with trees and bushes. Also heaths and young plantations.

Food: Insects; mainly beetles, flies and bugs. Lesser whitethroat prefers caterpillars. Berries in autumn.

Nest: Cup of grasses, lined with hair, low in dense vegetation. Built by male and lined by female.

Eggs: 4-5 (3-7). Green or grey with variable yellow or dark markings. Lesser whitethroat's are white with brown or grey marks. May-June. 2 clutches. Incubated for 12 days by both sexes.

Young: Nidicolous. Fed by both parents. Fly at 11 days.

In the field: Song. Grey cap of male. White throat. Raised crown feathers.

Whitethroat
♂

Lesser whitethroat
♂

Whitethroat

Lesser whitethroat

19 mm

17 mm

Garden Warbler
Sylvia borin

The garden warbler is the prototype 'little brown bird' and it has been said that it is best recognized by its lack of field marks. However, a trained eye can see particular features, such as the fine eyestripe, stubby bill, and the barely visible grey patch on the side of the head, although these are difficult to pick out as the bird slips through the foliage. As usual with warblers, the song is the best guide to identification, but, again, experience is needed to distinguish the garden warbler from the closely related blackcap. However, it is easy to tell these two apart by sight.

'Garden warbler' is not such a descriptive name as 'willow warbler'. Garden warblers are only likely to be seen in large gardens with shrubberies and bramble patches or in those close to woodland. They will, however, raid soft fruit crops such as currants, raspberries and cherries, as well as elder and other trees with berries, which provide a rich source of energy for the autumn migration.

○ Common.

○ Summer visitor.

○ British Isles, April-September.

○ Breeding, April-July.

○ Sexes similar.

○ Female blackcap has darker head.

Plumage: Uniformly dark brown head and upperparts with pale buff underparts. Faint white line over eye and grey patch on neck. Length 14 cm (5½ in).

Voice: A mellow, sustained warbling, less varied than blackcap.

Habitat: Large gardens, farms with overgrown hedges. Also young plantations and woodland.

Food: Insects; especially caterpillars. Fruit in late summer.

Nest: A cup of grasses lined with fine grass and hair. Built by both sexes.

Eggs: 4-6 (3-7). White with some olive or buff spots. May-June. Incubated for 10-11 days by both parents.

Young: Nidicolous. Fed by both parents. Fly at 15 days.

In the field: Plump shape, rounded head, uniform coloration.

Blackcap
Sylvia atricapilla

This is the most easily recognized warbler, provided there is the chance for a good look at its head. Its preferred habitat is woodland, and the blackcap usually only nests in gardens and farmland if there are trees and shrubs or tall hedgerows.

In recent years, the blackcap has become a garden bird, tempted by its new habit of feeding at birdtables. Like some other warblers, it turns from a diet of insects to fruit, as a means of laying down fat reserves for migration. The blackcap has broadened its diet to include the crumbs and scraps it can find on birdtables and, perhaps as a result of the great increase in these, has taken to wintering in Britain. This artificial supply of food helps to eke out the meagre winter stocks of berries and insects. Wintering birds are immigrants which have nested on the continent of Europe during the previous summer.

○ Common.

○ Summer visitor (and resident).

○ British Isles, March-October.

○ Breeding, March-June.

○ Males have black cap, females have brown cap.

Plumage: Upperparts greyish-brown. Sides of head and underparts grey. Male has black cap; female has brown cap. Juvenile similar to female. Length 14 cm (5½ in).

Voice: Shorter, more melodious and distinct warbling than garden warbler.

Habitat: Gardens and farms with undergrowth. Scrub around gravel pits. Also woodland.

Food: Insects, such as flies, caterpillars and beetles. Fruit and scraps.

Nest: Cup of grasses and roots, lined with fine grasses and feathers, usually sited higher than garden warblers. Built by both sexes.

Eggs: 4-5 (3-6). Buff with brown markings. April-June. 1-2 clutches. Incubated for 11 days by both parents.

Young: Nidicolous. Fed by both parents. Fly at 12 days.

In the field: Song. Grey plumage. Black cap of male, brown cap of female.

♀

♂

20 mm

Chiffchaff
Phylloscopus collybita

A few birds give away their names as soon as they are heard. The cuckoo is the obvious example, but the crow, peewit (or lapwing) curlew and chiffchaff also have onomatopoeic names. The steady *chiff-chaff-chiff-chaff* song of the chiffchaff rivals the popular cuckoo as a herald of spring, but few people recognize the rather dull warbler responsible for the sound.

The importance of birdsong in the recognition of birds is shown by the fact that the chiffchaff, willow warbler and wood warbler were not recognized as three distinct species until examined by the 18th-century naturalist, Gilbert White. Until then they had been known as willow-wrens. Gilbert White came to the conclusion that there were three species from the very different songs, and by slight differences in appearance. So slight are the physical differences that ornithologists refer to them as 'willowchiffs' if they can only see and not hear the birds.

○ Common.

○ Summer visitor.

○ British Isles, March-October.

○ Breeding, March-July.

○ Sexes similar.

○ Willow warbler greener above, yellower below and has pale legs.

○ Wood warbler more yellowish, with white belly. Yellow stripe over eye.

Plumage: Upperparts greenish-brown, underparts buff. Faint pale line over eye. Length 11 cm (4½ in).
Voice: A ringing, steady *chiff-chaff*, given in irregular order.
Habitat: Large gardens and parks with shrubberies. Farms with hedges and trees. Also woods and heaths.
Food: Insects; particularly flies and caterpillars.
Nest: A ball of leaves and stalks, with an entrance in the side and a lining of feathers. Built by the female.
Eggs: 5-6 (3-7). White with purplish spots. April-June. 1-2 clutches. Incubated for 13 days by female.
Young: Nidicolous. Fed by both parents. Fly at 14 days.
In the field: Song. Dark legs.

15 mm

Spotted Flycatcher
Muscicapa striata

Despite an unobtrusive, mousy appearance and a thin song which can be heard only at close quarters, the spotted flycatcher is a popular bird. Originally an inhabitant of woodland clearings and forest edges, it has found a new home on farmland where there are tree-lined hedgerows and small spinneys, and in mature gardens. It makes itself conspicuous through its habit of flying out from a perch to snap up insects with a great display of aerobatic skill. Because each bird has favourite perches they may easily be watched for long periods, especially if a pair is collecting food for youngsters. As the same nest site is used for several years, it is easy to keep watch for the return of known pairs.

The spotted flycatcher is a migrant and arrives in late spring. At first it may have to search for insects on vegetation or fly far and wide like a swallow. Only when flying insects become abundant can it take up position and wait for its prey to come within range.

○ Common.

○ Summer visitor.

○ British Isles, April-September.

○ Breeding, May-July.

○ Sexes similar.

Plumage: Greyish brown upperparts, whitish underparts. Head and breast are streaked. Juvenile more spotted than streaked. Length 14 cm (5½ in).
Voice: A thin, quiet squeaky song.
Habitat: Farms, gardens and parks. Also woods.
Food: Insects; especially flies, butterflies and wasps.
Nest: A delicate cup of moss and hair bound with cobwebs in a cranny, hole or ledge. Built by both sexes.
Eggs: 4-5 (2-6). Pale green with brown markings, densest at blunt end. May-June. 1-2 clutches. Incubated for 13 days by both sexes.
Young: Nidicolous. Fed by both parents. Fly at 13 days.
In the field: Streaky appearance. Flying out from perch.

adult

juvenile

19 mm

Long-tailed Tit
Aegithalos caudatus

Long-tailed tits are sufficiently different from other tits to be classed in a separate family. Like the true tits, they are agile birds that swing acrobatically among the twigs in search of insects, and the best time to see them is in the winter when the trees are bare. Small flocks of long-tailed tits flit from tree to tree, uttering quiet zi-zi and pit call notes. The species suffers enormously in hard winters but there is little that can be done since it does not readily come to birdtables. The tits try to keep warm on cold nights by huddling together.

Unlike the typical tit nest in a hole or nestbox, the long-tailed tit's nest is a marvellously constructed ball of moss and hair, bound together with cobwebs. The exterior is covered with lichen and the interior is lined with as many as 2,000 or more feathers. City-dwelling long-tailed tits substitute paper for the lichen. Sometimes other adults help the parents to rear the young.

○ Frequent.

○ Resident.

○ Breeding, March-June.

○ Sexes similar.

○ Pied wagtail is larger and spends most of time on the ground.

Plumage: Head dirty white with black bar above eye. Upperparts black with pinkish areas, especially on the rump. Underparts white with pinkish tinge especially on belly. Wings and tail black with white edging to feathers. Juvenile has darker head and no pink. Length 14 cm (5½ in). Tail 8 cm (3 in).

Voice: Thin zi-zi and soft pit calls.

Habitat: Farms, gardens and parks. Also woods and heaths.

Food: Insects, especially small moths, weevils and aphids. Spiders. Occasional seeds.

Nest: A hollow ball of moss, hair and cobwebs, lined with feathers and covered with lichen. Built by both sexes.

Eggs: 8-12. White with a few reddish spots. April-May. Incubated for 16 days by both sexes.

Young: Nidicolous. Fed by both parents, sometimes with additional helpers. Fly at 16 days.

In the field: Long tails, acrobatic habits. Black and white plumage.

14 mm

Marsh Tit
Parus palustris

The tits, short for titmice, are a popular, well-studied group of small birds; yet the marsh tit was only recognized as a species in 1900, when it was separated from the willow tit, *Parus montanus*. This is not surprising because the two still cause problems of identification. The name is also rather confusing because the marsh tit is not found in marshes but the name was coined before the species were separated: the willow tit prefers damper situations. The easiest way to identify the marsh tit is to listen for the *pitchou* song which is unlike anything in the willow tit's repertoire. There are also slight differences in appearance: the marsh tit has a smaller cap on the head and this is glossy black rather than dull chocolate. Another significant difference is that the marsh tit nests in natural holes which it can enlarge to suit its purposes, while the willow tit can excavate its own nestholes in rotten wood.

○ Frequent.

○ Resident.

○ Breeding, March-June.

○ Sexes similar.

○ Willow tit has chocolate cap extending down nape and light patch on closed wing.

○ Coal tit has white nape on black head.

Plumage: Upperparts brown, underparts greyish. Cap glossy black, cheeks white, chin black. Juvenile more greyish above and whiter below, cap browner. Length 11 cm (4½ in).

Voice: *Pitchou* followed by harsh, scolding notes.

Habitat: Woodland. Also farms, parks and gardens.

Food: Mainly insects, such as weevils. Also beechmast, berries and seeds.

Nest: Pile of moss, topped with hair and feathers in a natural hole. Built by female.

Eggs: 7-9 (5-11). White with few brown spots. April-May. Incubated for 14 days by female.

Young: Nidicolous. Fed by both parents. Fly at 16 days.

In the field: *Pitchou* notes. Glossy black cap.

16 mm

Blue Tit
Parus caeruleus

The blue tit is *the* birdtable bird. It is the only tit to take large quantities of crumbs and its acrobatic ability makes it the main visitor to hanging food-dispensers. The number of blue tits that can come into the garden was only fully demonstrated by bird-ringing. Although no more than four or five are seen at one time, several hundred blue tits can visit one birdtable over the course of a single day. Woodland blue tits commute into towns to feed in winter and some stay to roost in streetlamps.

The charm of watching these blue and yellow acrobats is rather offset by their occasional attacks on human property. They tear open milk bottle tops to drink the cream in cold weather and, in their search for food, peck at the putty around windowpanes, or indulge in sporadic outbreaks of wallpaper tearing. Blue tits can also be pests in gardens and orchards when they attack peas, flowers and fruit.

○ Common.

○ Resident.

○ Breeding, January-June.

○ Sexes similar.

○ Other tits have black on the crown.

Plumage: Back yellow-green, wings and tail blue.
Underparts yellow.
Crown blue. Face white bordered by dark line from chin and through eyes. Juveniles have yellow replacing white on head. Length 11 cm (4½ in).
Voice: A trilling, repeated two-note *twee-soo*.
Habitat: Woodland. Also farms, parks and gardens.
Food: Insects, especially caterpillars and weevils. Also fruit and buds.
Nest: Moss and grass lined with feathers or hair, in a natural hole or nestbox. Built by both sexes.
Eggs: 10-12 (4-17). White with brown spots. April-June.
Incubated for 14 days by female.
Young: Nidicolous. Fed by both parents. Fly at 19 days.
In the field: Blue and yellow plumage.

15 mm

Great Tit
Parus major

The strikingly marked great tit is the bully of the family, and at the birdtable can be seen displacing smaller birds from the food. If necessary, it fans its tail, half-spreads its wings and gapes at its rivals. Blue tits use this display much less frequently. Great tits are rather less acrobatic than other tits but can cling agilely to a string of peanuts. However, they tend to keep away from the finer twigs and regularly descend to the ground to feed, coming on to lawns and fields. They are strong enough to hack open hazel nuts and sometimes attack bees.

The great tit's song is the familiar *teacher-teacher* which gave the bird its old country name of 'saw-sharpener'. It has a wide range of variations to this song, as well as many other calls. Forty different calls have been recorded from a single bird and it is often said that any unfamiliar bird sound heard in the countryside is probably made by a great tit.

○ Common.

○ Resident.

○ Breeding, January-July.

○ Males have broader stripe on belly.

○ Blue tit lacks black head and belly.

Plumage: Back green, wings and tail grey-blue with white outer tail feathers and wing bar. Underparts yellow with broad black band. Head black with white cheeks. Female has narrower band on belly. Juvenile is paler. Length 14 cm (5½ in).
Voice: *Chink* call and *teacher-teacher* song.
Habitat: Woodland. Also farms, parks and gardens.
Food: Insects, especially weevils and caterpillars. Fruit and buds.
Nest: Moss lined with hair in a natural hole or nestbox. Built by both sexes.
Eggs: 5-12 (5-18). White with sparse brown markings. April-June. Incubated for 14 days by female.
Young: Nidicolous. Fed by both parents. Fly at 20 days.
In the field: Song. Yellow underparts and black stripe.

♀

♂

18 mm

Red-backed Shrike
Lanius collurio

This is an interesting species which has unfortunately become much less familiar in recent years. Fifty years ago there were red-backed shrikes over most of England and Wales but they are now rare and there are only around 35 pairs left. Most of these are in Norfolk, Suffolk, Surrey and Hampshire.

Shrikes behave like miniature hawks and at one time they were trained for falconry. They wait on a perch with a good view or fly along hedges, then swoop out to catch insects or even larger animals. The strong hooked bill is used for killing the prey which may then be carried in the feet.

Surplus prey is stored in a 'larder', where the shrike impales its victims on thorns or barbed wire. Sometimes they are eaten at a later date but often they are left and the habit has earned the red-backed shrike the nickname of 'butcherbird'.

○ Rare.

○ Summer visitor.

○ British Isles, April-September.

○ Breeding, May-July.

○ Male more colourful.

○ Wheatear grey on back and white rump.

○ Spotted flycatcher has similar hunting method but has grey streaked appearance.

Plumage: Male has chestnut back and wings, grey crown, neck and rump. There is a broad black stripe through the eyes. Underparts white with a pink tinge. Tail black with white edges. Female is a general dull brown above, buffish with crescent-shaped markings below and some grey on the head. Juvenile like female with more distinct crescent markings. Length 18 cm (7 in).

Voice: Harsh *chack-chack* and a quiet warbling song.

Habitat: Heathland. Formerly downs, farmland and gardens.

Food: Insects, especially beetles and bumblebees. Also small birds and mammals, reptiles and worms.

Nest: Grasses and moss, lined with rootlets and hair. Built mainly by male.

Eggs: 4-6 (3-7). Very variable, pink, brown, green or white with dark markings. May-July. Incubated for 14 days mainly by female.

Young: Nidicolous. Fed by both parents. Fly at 14 days.

In the field: Grey and chestnut, with black eyestripe of male. Larder.

23 mm

Magpie
Pica pica

Quite unmistakable with its black and white plumage and long tail, even when hidden the magpie's presence is given away by its loud raucous calls. Its old name was simply 'pie', after its pied pattern. 'Magpie' is short for 'maggot pie', itself an abbreviation of 'Margaret pie'. Other birds with 'Christian names' include Robin redbreast, Tom tit and Jackdaw.

Magpies used to be linked with witchcraft and bad luck, and their habit of raiding birds' nests led to their being persecuted by gamekeepers. They became very scarce in many places but their numbers have now increased. Magpies are now nesting in cities such as London and Birmingham and they occasionally come to birdtables to feed.

There is a popular rhyme that tells your fortune depending on the number of magpies seen: 'One's sorrow, two's mirth' and so on. Sometimes scores of magpies gather together, although the reason is not known.

○ Frequent.

○ Resident.

○ Breeding, March-July.

○ Sexes similar.

○ Pied wagtail very much smaller.

Plumage: Contrasting black and white. The white is on the belly, flanks and in a V across the back. The wings are iridescent blue and the tail iridescent green. Juvenile duller. Length 46 cm (18 in).
Voice: A harsh chatter.
Habitat: Farmland with hedgerows. Parks and gardens. Also woods and cliffs.
Food: Mainly insects but also other invertebrates, eggs and small birds and mammals. Grain, nuts, fruit and other vegetables.
Nest: Bulky construction of twigs lined with earth and rootlets and roofed with dome of twigs. Built by both sexes.
Eggs: 5-7 (2-8). Greenish or greyish with close dark spots. April-May. Incubated for 17 days by female.
Young: Nidicolous. Fed by both parents. Fly at 27 days.
In the field: Black and white plumage. Long tail. Call.

34 mm

Jackdaw
Corvus monedula

Jackdaws have had a long association with humans because they often nest in chimneys or ruined buildings. They are sometimes not welcome since their nests block chimneys and many twigs fall into the fireplace before enough get firmly wedged to make a foundation for the nest. Jackdaws have also been responsible for setting fire to houses by carrying burning embers to their nests. This was quite a frequent occurrence when thatched houses and open fires were common. They are curious birds and have the habit of collecting or playing with bright objects.

Jackdaws are very sociable, living in flocks and nesting in colonies of varying density. When one member of the flock is attacked, the others go to its assistance. The bond between a pair is strong and they can be seen keeping close together in a flock. The pair seem to be very affectionate; they stay together all year and probably mate for life.

○ Common.

○ Resident.

○ Breeding, April-June.

○ Sexes similar.

○ Rook larger and with white at base of bill.

○ Carrion crow and raven larger and all black.

Plumage: Glossy black with a bluish tinge, except for silver grey on the nape and sides of the head. Juveniles duller with grey less contrasting. Length 33 cm (13 in).
Voice: Sharp *tchack* or *kyow*.
Habitat: Farmland, towns and gardens. Also woods and cliffs.
Food: Mainly insects, with other invertebrates and occasionally small birds and mammals. Grain, fruit and other vegetables.
Nest: A mass of twigs in a cavity in a tree, building or rock. Lined with mud, bark and hair. Built by both sexes.
Eggs: 4-5 (3-7). Pale bluish green with dark specks. April-May. Incubated for 19 days by female.
Young: Nidicolous. Fed by both parents. Fly at 32 days.
In the field: Small size and grey nape. Calls.

adult

juvenile

36 mm

Rook
Corvus frugilegus

The rookery in a clump of tall trees in a village or on a farm is a familiar country sight. The large nests of twigs are very conspicuous in winter and the rooks can be seen there for much of the year. A chorus of harsh cawing accompanies their courtship and disputes over the ownership of nests. During nest building the female stays nearby to prevent other rooks from stealing sticks from it.

Sometimes the whole flock takes off and flies around. This may be caused by a sudden alarm but at other times the rooks circle around each other and seem to be thoroughly enjoying themselves playing in the breeze.

It used to be believed by country people that rooks occasionally held a 'parliament' in which a 'criminal' rook was condemned and pecked to death. The explanation seems to be that rooks may attack injured or otherwise abnormal companions.

○ Common.

○ Resident.

○ Breeding, March-June.

○ Sexes similar.

○ Carrion crow and raven lack bare face and leggings.

○ Jackdaw has grey nape and is smaller.

Plumage: All black with a purplish gloss. Grey area bare of feathers around base of bill. Juvenile duller. Length 46 cm (18 in).
Voice: A harsh *kaah*.
Habitat: Farmland and villages. Also moors and heaths.
Food: Earthworms and grain. Also other insects and invertebrates, small birds and mammals. Many other kinds of vegetable food.
Nest: Sticks lined with earth and leaves. Built by both sexes.
Eggs: 3-5 (2-9). Light green with brown speckles. March-April. Incubated for 17 days by female.
Young: Nidicolous. Fed by both parents. Fly at 32 days.
In the field: Pale grey bare skin on face, giving effect of high forehead. Shaggy 'leggings' on thighs.

juvenile

adult

40 mm

Carrion/Hooded Crow
Corvus corone

Over much of Britain, the familiar crow is a bird with uniformly black plumage but in the western Highlands of Scotland, on the Isle of Man and in Ireland it is replaced by the hooded crow which has a grey body. The two birds are subspecies of the same species and have identical calls and behaviour. Where they overlap in Scotland they interbreed and produce hybrids. The range of the carrion crow has been moving northwards recently, especially in eastern Scotland.

It is sometimes said that crows are seen in ones and twos, whereas rooks live in flocks, but this is not an infallible guide to identification. Crows sometimes gather in small groups.

Crows, like their relatives, are intelligent and adaptable birds. They make use of a wide variety of foods – carrion is less important than the name suggests. Pairs of crows sometimes co-operate to rob gulls, herons or birds of prey.

Hooded crow   Carrion crow

○ Common.

○ Resident.

○ Breeding, April-July.

○ Sexes similar.

○ Rook has bare pale grey face and 'leggings'.

○ Raven is larger with wedge-shaped tail.

○ Jackdaw smaller with grey nape.

Plumage: All black with a bluish gloss. Hooded crow has grey body and underside of wings. Juvenile duller. Length 46 cm (18 in).
Voice: Harsh *kaaa*, usually given 3 or 4 times.
Habitat: Farmland, parks and towns. Also woodland, moors, coasts.
Food: A very wide variety of animal and plant food, including carrion and refuse, small birds and mammals, fish and shellfish.
Nest: Sticks, heather or seaweed in a tree, telegraph pole or electricity pylon, lined with earth, bark, roots, grass and hair. Built by both sexes.
Eggs: 4-5 (2-7). Pale green with olive-brown speckles and blotches. April-May. Incubated for 18 days by female.
Young: Nidicolous. Fed by both parents. Fly at 34 days.
In the field: All black plumage, or grey body. Square rather than rounded tip to tail.

Hooded crow

adult

adult

Carrion crow

43 mm

Starling
Sturnus vulgaris

If you walk through crowded streets on a winter's evening, look up, and you may see streams of starlings flying in to roost on buildings and trees. Starlings have become a problem in towns and cities because their droppings foul buildings and defoliate trees. They are also a nuisance because they take over the nests of woodpeckers, martins and other birds and greedily clear birdtables before other species can get a meal.

Starlings have been introduced to other parts of the world, including America, and have become a pest there. It seems strange that such an unprepossessing bird should be spread deliberately but, seen close to, a starling's plumage is by no means drab, being shot with green and purple. The bird is also a good mimic. It regularly imitates other birds such as curlews, lapwings and chickens, as well as foxes, human whistles and telephone bells.

○ Common.

○ Resident.

○ Breeding, April-June.

○ Female more spotted.

○ Thrushes brown above, pale with spots below.

Plumage: Black with buffish marks above and whitish marks below. Greenish and purplish sheen. Winter plumage less glossy and with grey speckling on head and underparts. Female more spotted. Bill greyish-brown in winter, adult's yellow in summer. Juvenile grey-brown with white throat. Length 20 cm (8 in).

Voice: A grating *cheer* and a rambling warbling with a variety of whistles, clicks and mimicking.

Habitat: Farms, gardens and cities. Also woods and moors.

Food: Insects and other invertebrates. Many kinds of vegetable food, including seeds and berries.

Nest: In hole in tree, building or among boulders. Sometimes other birds' nests. Untidy mass of dry grasses, lined with feathers. Built by male.

Eggs: 5-7 (4-9). Pale blue. April-May. 1-2 clutches. Incubated for 12 days by both sexes.

Young: Nidicolous. Fed by both parents. Fly at 21 days.

In the field: Speckled plumage. Tight flocks in flight. Single bird looks like flying arrowhead.

juvenile

adult

30 mm

House Sparrow
Passer domesticus

The house sparrow is not the most common bird in the country since it depends on human beings. Both chaffinch and blackbird are more numerous. House sparrows probably arrived in Britain only when agriculture started in Neolithic times and in the countryside they survive on grain crops or food of farm animals. In towns they used to live on spilt grain but, when horses were replaced by cars and lorries, sparrows came to rely heavily on birdtables and the increasing amount of litter.

House sparrows can cause serious damage to crops and gardeners dislike them for their habit of pecking the leaves of crocuses and primulas, especially yellow varieties. They also offend some bird lovers by nesting in boxes put up for tits and usurping house martin nests. The nest is often used as a roost in winter and the constant chirping heard in spring is the sign of a male advertising his nesting place to unattached females.

○ Common.

○ Resident.

○ Breeding, March-August.

○ Female lacks black throat.

○ Tree sparrow has brown cap and black spot on white cheek.

○ Dunnock has grey underparts.

○ Reed bunting has black head and white neck.

Plumage: Male brown with black streaks above and greying cheeks and underparts. Black on throat and in front of eyes. Grey crown. White wing bar. Grey rump. Female and juvenile duller, lacking black throat, grey crown and rump. Length 15 cm (6 in).
Voice: Various *cheep* and twittering calls.
Habitat: Towns and farmland. Nests in cavity in building or tree, other bird's nest or in hedge.
Food: Mainly grains and weed seeds. Also some insects and buds.
Nest: Untidy dome of straws, with hole in side. Lined with feathers. Built by both sexes.
Eggs: 3-5 (7). Greyish-white with darker grey or brown spots. April-August. 3 clutches. Incubated for 13 days mainly by female.
Young: Nidicolous. Fed by both parents. Fly at 15 days.
In the field: Black throat, grey cheeks of male. Tame urban dweller.

♂

♀

23 mm

Tree Sparrow
Passer montanus

Less tied to human habitation and activities, tree sparrows are to be seen over most of England, Wales and southern Scotland but they are usually overlooked. Their overall appearance is very similar to house sparrows but they are slimmer and the sexes are similar. The two species often mix together and the tree sparrow's presence may be recognized by its different calls as well as by its appearance. Their diets are similar but tree sparrows eat more insects than house sparrows, especially outside the breeding season.

Tree sparrows usually nest in holes such as those in pollarded willows, or in woodpecker holes and will make use of nestboxes. They are slender enough to get into boxes which have entrances narrow enough to exclude house sparrows. Nests are sometimes made in dense hedgerows and a surprising nesting place is underneath occupied rooks' nests. Apart from the solid security of the larger birds' constructions, the sparrows have the added bonus of being able to gather scraps dropped by the rooks.

○ Frequent.

○ Resident.

○ Breeding, April-August.

○ Sexes similar.

○ House sparrow has black bib and grey crown and rump. Sexes different.

○ Dunnock has grey underparts.

○ Reed bunting has black head and white neck.

Plumage: Dark brown with black streaks above. Cheeks and underparts greyish-white. Chestnut-brown head. Black chin and in front of eyes. Black spot on cheek. White wing bar. Length 13 cm (5 in).

Voice: *Cheep* higher pitched than house sparrow's. *Teck-teck* in flight. Chirping song.

Habitat: Parks and gardens, farmland. Also woods and cliffs.

Food: Insects, grains and seeds of weeds.

Nest: Dried grasses in hole; domed if in open. Built by both sexes.

Eggs: 3-5 (2-8). White with fine brown markings. April-July. 2-3 clutches. Incubated for 13 days by both parents.

Young: Nidicolous. Fed by both parents. Fly at 14 days.

In the field: Black cheek spot, brown head. White collar. Call.

19 mm

Chaffinch
Fringilla coelebs

The chaffinch is one of the commonest birds in Britain. It is found wherever there are trees and bushes for the neatly woven nest and suitable perch for the singing male. Numbers decreased, however, during the 1950s, probably through the effects of poisoning by agricultural seed dressings.

The tinkling song with its terminal flourish is a familiar sound in early spring, and travellers with a good ear and memory will notice that the pattern of the song changes across the country. It is partly instinctive and partly learned by the young bird listening to neighbouring adults, so that birds in one locality tend to develop a dialect.

Every autumn the British population is swollen by immigrants coming from Scandinavia. The natives tend to spend the winter around their old territories but the immigrants gather to feed in flocks in fields and retire to roost communally in woods.

○ Common.

○ Resident, with winter visitors.

○ Breeding, March-July.

○ Female lacks blue head and pink breast.

○ Brambling has white patch on back but no white on tail.

Plumage: Male in summer is chestnut on the back, green on the rump and grey on the tail coverts. Tail is black with white edges. Wings have two white bars. Crown and nape blue. Cheeks, throat and breast pink, becoming paler on the belly. In winter the head is buffish red and the back is paler chestnut. Female is duller, lacking the blue on the head and pink on the face and breast. Juvenile is like female. Length 15 cm (6 in).
Voice: *Pink-pink* call. Song is a series of notes ending with a flourish.
Habitat: Parks, gardens and farms. Nests in trees and bushes.
Food: Mainly seeds; also insects, especially caterpillars.
Nest: A neat cup of grasses, lined with hair and decorated with lichens. Built by female.
Eggs: 4-5 (3-6). Green-blue with purple-brown spots and streaks, each having a lighter border. April-June. Incubated for 13 days by female.
Young: Nidicolous. Fed by both parents. Fly at 14 days.
In the field: Male's blue head. White on wings and tail. Call and song.

♂

♀

20 mm

Brambling
Fringilla montifringilla

The brambling is a winter visitor to Britain although there is one record of nesting in Scotland. It is remarkably like the chaffinch in its habits except that it breeds farther north, in Scandinavia and Siberia. There is only a narrow strip of country where the brambling and the chaffinch nest together.

After their arrival in Britain, bramblings often form into flocks with chaffinches, moving and flying together almost as one species. Both enjoy similar types of food but bramblings are very fond of beechmast and will travel far in search of a good crop. However, they may join the chaffinches to feed in fields. On their return north, bramblings sometimes stop off for a while in conifer woods.

Migrations are erratic from year to year. Bramblings which have spent one winter in Britain may travel to central or southern Europe in the next.

○ Scarce.

○ Winter visitor.

○ British Isles, September-April.

○ Does not nest in British Isles.

○ Female has grey nape.

○ Male chaffinch has pink breast, brown back and white on tail.

Plumage: The male in winter is orange-buff with mottled buff head and back, and white belly. There is a distinct white patch on the lower rump. Bright yellow under wing. In summer the head and back become black. The female is paler with a grey-brown head and a black stripe behind the eyes. Juveniles are still paler. Length 15 cm (6 in).
Voice: A hoarse *tsweek* and a repeated *chuck-chuck* in flight.
Habitat: Fields and farmyards. Also woods.
Food: Beechmast, seeds of weeds and grain, conifer seeds. Insects, especially caterpillars.
Nest: Grass, lined with feathers and camouflaged with lichen and bark. Built by female.
Eggs: 6-7 (4-8). Similar to chaffinches, but sometimes greener. May-July. Incubated for 14 days by the female.
Young: Nidicolous. Fed by both parents. Fly at 14 days.
In the field: Orange plumage. White patch on rump. Calls.

♀ winter

♂ winter

19 mm

Greenfinch
Carduelis chloris

Greenfinches have benefited enormously from birdtables. Their diet is mainly seeds; in summer they feed on the seeds of elm and dog's mercury in woods and many weed seeds and grains from standing crops. Autumn sees a turn to feeding on yew and brambles. At one time hard weather drove greenfinches to look for food in farmyards where grain had been spilt during threshing. Nowadays they come into gardens and especially take advantage of the peanuts hanging in bags and feeders. Before they learned to feed on peanuts, green-finches stripped the fruit from garden shrubs such as *Daphne mezereum*. This habit started more than 100 years ago in the north of England and has spread through Britain and across the Continent.

Winter nights are spent in communal roosts among evergreen shrubs. There may be several hundred, even as many as 2,000, birds in one gathering. Nesting is also sociable with several pairs breeding close together.

○ Common.

○ Resident.

○ Breeding, April-August.

○ Female duller.

○ Serin much smaller, with streaked back.

○ Siskin much smaller, with yellow and black wings.

Plumage: Male is olive-green with greenish-yellow breast and rump, and bright yellow flashes on wings and sides of tail. Female is more brown with less yellow. Juvenile like female, with streaks. Length 15 cm (6 in).

Voice: Drawn-out *tsweee* and a rapid twitter.

Habitat: Gardens and parks with plenty of shrubs. Nests in bushes and hedges. Farmland with hedges and copses. Also woods.

Food: Mainly a variety of seeds and grains. Some insects, especially caterpillars and aphids.

Nest: Twigs, grass and moss lined with hair and rootlets. Built by both sexes.

Eggs: 4-6 (3-7). White to pale blue with red-brown spots. April-August. 2-3 clutches. Incubated for 13 days by female.

Young: Nidicolous. Fed by both parents. Fly at 16 days.

In the field: Green and yellow plumage. Call.

21 mm

Goldfinch
Carduelis carduelis

FINCHES
Fringillidae

The goldfinch might claim to be the prettiest of Britain's native birds and a flock deserves its old name of a 'charm of goldfinches'. Unfortunately for the goldfinch, its patchwork of bright colours and its pleasant liquid song made it a popular cagebird. In Victorian times, people made a living selling the hundreds of thousands of goldfinches trapped every year. It was particularly easy to catch them on their migration routes, and saving the goldfinch was one of the first priorities when the Royal Society for the Protection of Birds was formed in 1889.

The best time to see goldfinches is in the late summer and autumn when small flocks roam the countryside and gather on the dead stems of thistles, dandelions, ragwort and similar plants. The goldfinch's slender bill is adept at picking out seeds deeply embedded in the seed-heads and it is the only finch which can extract the well-hidden seeds of teazel.

○ Common.

○ Resident.

○ Breeding, March-August.

○ Female duller.

○ Siskin lacks red and white on head.

Plumage: Back and flanks chestnut, belly and rump white. Wings and tail black with broad yellow bar on wing and white markings on edge of wing and tail. Head black and white with red around bill. Female duller with less red on face. Juvenile streaked, with no black, white and red on head. Length 13 cm (5 in).

Voice: A liquid *tswitt-witt-witt*.

Habitat: Gardens, parks and farms with trees and weed patches. Nests high and far out on boughs. Also woods.

Food: Seeds, mainly of thistles and related weeds. Also birch, alder and pine. Some insects.

Nest: Deep cup of moss, roots, lichen and wool. Lined with thistledown. Built by female.

Eggs: 4-6 (3-7). White with a few brown streaks. May-August. 2-3 clutches. Incubated for 12 days by female.

Young: Nidicolous. Fed by both parents. Fly at 14 days.

In the field: Yellow on wings. Black, white and red on head.

juvenile

adult

17 mm

Linnet
Carduelis cannabina

Like the goldfinch, the linnet was once so popular as a cagebird that its numbers were reduced in the wild. Although the cock linnet's plumage is delicately attractive, it was kept for its voice. The song of a linnet does not carry far but is cheerfully musical with its medley of harp- and flute-like notes. Sometimes several males sing in chorus.

Linnets used to be crossed with canaries in the belief that the offspring would sing better than either parent. They were also kept with other birds because the linnet's song is partly learned by listening to them. In nature, they learn from other linnets but they can be persuaded to adopt other songs in captivity.

Although common, linnets are easily overlooked especially when they flock with other more recognizable finches. They rarely come into suburban gardens in Britain, but they do nest in towns in Sweden and Finland.

○ Common.

○ Resident.

○ Breeding, March-July.

○ Female lacks crimson.

○ Twite has less white on wings and tail. Male has crimson rump.

○ Redpoll has black chin.

Plumage: Male has chestnut-brown upperparts with white on the wings and tail. Head greyish brown. Forehead and breast crimson. Female lacks crimson. Juvenile like female but with more streaking. Length 13 cm (5 in).
Voice: Metallic *chi-chi-chi-chi* in flight. Song is a varied selection of twanging and fluting notes.
Habitat: Farmland with rough ground and stubble. Commons. Nests low in bushes. Also seashores.
Food: Seeds, mainly of weeds and the members of the cabbage family. Some insects.
Nest: Twigs, grasses and moss, lined with hair. Built by female.
Eggs: 4-6 (7). Bluish-white with purplish-red streaks and spots. April-July. 2-3 clutches. Incubated for 12 days, mainly by female.
Young: Nidicolous. Fed by both parents. Fly at 12 days.
In the field: Chestnut back and crimson breast of male. Song.

♂

♀

18 mm

Bullfinch
Pyrrhula pyrrhula

The bullfinch is another species that was once a popular cagebird. It is colourful but its song is quiet and unassuming. Its attraction is that it is a ready mimic. The poet William Cowper wrote of bullfinches:

And though by nature mute
Or only with a whistle blessed,
Well taught he all the sounds expressed
Of flageolet or flute.

'Bird flageolets' were frequently used for teaching birds to whistle tunes and one bullfinch was taught the National Anthem.

Today bullfinches are unfortunately better known as pests in orchards. For much of the year they feed on seeds but they descend on buds and flowers of trees and bushes in spring. Branches are systematically stripped and a single bullfinch can destroy 30 buds in a minute. Entire crops can be lost in bad 'bullfinch years'.

⦿ Common.

⦿ Resident.

⦿ Breeding, April-August.

⦿ Female lacks pink breast.

⦿ Hawfinch lacks black cap and white rump.

⦿ Wheatear lacks black cap.

Plumage: Blue-grey back with black wings and tail. Grey bar on wings. White rump. Cheek and breast pink. Crown black. Female has grey-brown back and breast. Juvenile lacks black cap. Length 15 cm (6 in).

Voice: Piping whistle. Quiet creaking song.

Habitat: Parks, gardens and farmland with hedgerows. Nests in hedges and bushes. Also woods.

Food: Mainly seeds such as dog's mercury, birch, bramble, dock, nettle and ash. Buds and flowers of oak, hawthorn and fruit trees. Also some insects.

Nest: Base of twigs with rootlets, moss and lichen. Built by both sexes.

Eggs: 4-5 (3-7). Greenish white with a few spots and streaks of purplish brown. April-July. 2-3 clutches. Incubated for 13 days mainly by female.

Young: Nidicolous. Fed by both parents. Fly at 16 days.

In the field: Black cap, wings and tail. White rump. Pink breast of male. Call.

♀

♂

20 mm

Yellowhammer
Emberiza citrinella

The yellowhammer or yellow bunting is famous for singing 'Little-bit-of-bread-and-no-cheese'. This is one of the familiar summer sounds in the countryside where there is open ground with scattered bushes and hedges. Consequently, yellowhammers are found on farms, commons, heaths and in young plantations of trees where there is still open ground and some bushes or brambles. Open ground is needed for feeding on fallen seeds and small animals; undergrowth is required for nesting and trees for singing. Telegraph wires are an acceptable substitute for trees as singing posts.

During the winter, yellowhammers band together in flocks, which can often be seen in stubble fields. These start to break up in February and males become separated, each one advertising its territory by singing from perches and attacking other male yellowhammers.

- ◯ Common.
- ◯ Resident.
- ◯ Breeding, February-August.
- ◯ Female less yellow.
- ◯ Cirl bunting has black chin.

Plumage: Male has chestnut upperparts streaked with black except on rump. White edges on tail. Head and underparts yellow. Female has less yellow. Juvenile darker. Length 17 cm (6½ in).
Voice: *Twick* and *twit-up* calls. Song is 'Little-bit-of-bread-and-no-cheese'.
Habitat: Farmland, commons and heaths. Nest on or near ground under cover.
Food: Weed seeds, grain and some fruit. Small insects and other invertebrates.
Nest: Grasses and moss, lined with fine grass and hair. Built by female.
Eggs: 3-4 (2-6). White to brownish with many fine brown lines. April-August. 2-3 clutches. Incubated for 13 days by female.
Young: Nidicolous. Fed by both parents. Fly at 13 days.
In the field: Yellow head and underparts. Song.

22 mm

Reed Bunting
Emberiza schoeniclus

Until a few years ago, the reed bunting lived up to its name, nesting in reedbeds and other swampy vegetation growing in and around water. Ornithologists noted that reed buntings did not trespass on the surrounding drier land which was the preserve of yellowhammers and corn buntings. About 50 years ago, a few reed buntings started to nest in drier places and the habit has spread. It appears that, during the late 1960s, the reed bunting population was high, while yellowhammers had become fewer so that the extra reed buntings could move from the wetlands. At the same time wet places were dwindling as more land was drained and ploughed. Nowadays reed buntings can be heard singing even in the middle of large barley fields.

A second change of habit is the appearance of reed buntings on birdtables in winter. At this time of year the males have lost the distinctive black and white plumage on the head.

- Frequent.

- Resident.

- Breeding, March-July.

- Female lacks black and white colouring on head.

- House sparrow lacks white edges of tail. Male's head less distinctive.

- Stonechat has chestnut breast.

- Blackcap has plain brown and grey plumage and less black on head.

Plumage: Male in summer has brown upperparts with black streaks. Head is black with collar and 'moustache'. Rump grey. Edges of tail white. Underparts buff streaked with black. In winter the pattern of black and white on the head is obscured by buff. Female resembles male in winter. Juvenile like female with more streaking above and yellowish tinge below. Length 15 cm (6 in).

Voice: Shrill *chit* of alarm. Song is a repeated, monotonous *tweek-tweek-tweek-tititick*.

Habitat: Wet places, farmland, gardens in winter, downs and waste ground. Nests on or near ground in cover. Also coastal dunes, moors and young plantations.

Food: Seeds of marsh plants, grasses and weeds. Also insects and other invertebrates.

Nest: Grasses with lining of finer grass and hair, built by female.

Eggs: 4-5 (7). Brownish-green with large dark brown spots and streaks. April-June. 2-3 clutches. Incubated for 14 days by female.

Young: Nidicolous. Fed by both parents. Fly at 12 days.

In the field: Black and white head. White edges of tail. Song.

20 mm

Corn Bunting
Emberiza calandra

The corn bunting's name reflects its link with farming and, although it can be found on downs and rough grasslands, it is among arable crops and hay that this species must be sought. Throughout the spring and summer, the rattling song – likened to 'a jangling bunch of keys' – can be heard coming monotonously, hour after hour, from the fields. The male corn bunting sings from a perch as tall as an electricity pylon or as low as a stone. Without this characteristic song, corn buntings could be mistaken easily for female house sparrows, meadow pipits or other small brown birds, especially when they flock in winter. Another distinguishing feature is the male's habit of circling or hovering very low with his legs dangling.

Corn buntings are rather unusual buntings in several respects. The most important is that they are polygamous. One male may mate with up to seven females, each of whom rears a family.

○ Frequent.

○ Resident.

○ Breeding, February-August.

○ Sexes similar.

○ Skylark has slight crest, heavily streaked breast, white on tail.

○ Meadow pipit has white streak above eye and white on tail.

○ Female house sparrow uniformly brown underneath.

Plumage: Brown with short dark streaks above. Underparts buff with dark streaks, making an almost solid patch on breast. Length 18 cm (7 in).
Voice: Repeated *quit-quit-quit* in flight. Song sound like 'a jangling bunch of keys'.
Habitat: Farms and grasslands.
Food: Mainly seeds, with some leaves and buds. Also some insects and other invertebrates.
Nest: Grasses, with a lining of finer grasses and rootlets. Built by female.
Eggs: 3-5 (1-7). Dirty white with thick dark brown lines and spots. May-July. 2 clutches. Incubated for 12 days by the female.
Young: Nidicolous. Fed by female. Fly at 10 days.
In the field: Song. Pattern on breast. Lack of white tail feathers.

24 mm

Conservation

The various species of British countryside birds have been subjected to a variety of pressures. The planting of hedges about 200 years ago led to an increase in many songbirds, whereas the rearing of game-birds prompted a huge persecution of birds of prey. Egg collecting was once a popular pastime and it is not generally realized that, in Victorian times, huge numbers of small birds were trapped for eating or for keeping as cagebirds. Periods of hard weather, such as the winter of 1962-3, have also had their effect on the populations of the smaller birds of Great Britain.

The fortunes of birds are still fluctuating as attempts are made to conserve them on the one hand, while changes in the countryside threaten them on the other. The first law for protecting wild birds was the Act for the Preservation of Seabirds passed in 1869. A general Wild Birds Protection Act followed in 1880 and the situation today is that nearly all birds are protected. The exceptions are the gamebirds and some birds which are pests. It is also illegal to steal eggs and to disturb the nests of rare species. Legal protection means that most birds are safe, but in some places birds of prey are still threatened by unscrupulous gamekeepers and collectors.

The changes in the countryside are a greater threat to birds and other kinds of animals. Old woods are cut down; bare hills and heaths are planted with conifers; hedgerows, ponds, pastures and marshes disappear under the plough; and roads and buildings continue to spread. Some birds can adapt to the new conditions but others need a particular habitat for survival. If this goes, they disappear. Birds are also threatened by the increased use of pesticides. They may eat grain treated with poisonous chemicals, or insects which have already picked up poisons. Pesticides accumulate in the birds' bodies to kill them or render them infertile, and the wholesale slaughter of insects destroys some birds' food supply. Seabirds face the additional danger of oilspills from tankers and installations.

Conservation means more than protecting birds by law. The environment must be preserved so that birds can live safely. Oilspills must be prevented and the use of pesticides reduced or made safer. For example, pesticides can be made less toxic to birdlife or applied in such a way that birds are less likely to pick them up. It is even more necessary that key habitats be preserved. Many areas of woodland, moor, heath and marsh have now been turned into nature reserves. Some, like those belonging to the Royal Society for the Protection of Birds, are managed primarily for birds. Outside the reserves, birds can be conserved by leaving trees, hedges and ponds, or patches of waste ground, so that there are places in which they can feed and nest.

Protection by law and creation of reserves will not save our birds unless people appreciate them. Education is a very important part of conservation; we must be made to understand that birds, and all wildlife, are worth preserving for the future.

Organizations

British Naturalists' Association,
Willowfield, Boyneswood Road,
Four Marks, Alton, Hants.
Supports schemes for maintaining
the beauty of the countryside and
establishing nature reserves.

The British Trust for Ornithology,
Beech Grove, Tring, Hertfordshire.
Organizes censuses, ringing and
other field studies.

Countryside Commission,
1 Cambridge Gate, Regent's Park,
London NW1 4JY. Responsible for
national parks and other amenities
for enjoying the countryside.

**Fauna and Flora Preservation
Society,** c/o Zoological Society of
London, Regent's Park, London
NW1 4RY. Promotes the
conservation of plants and
animals.

National Trust, 42 Queen Anne's
Gate, London SW1H 9AS.
Preserves land and buildings of
historic interest or national beauty.

The Nature Conservancy Council,
19-20 Belgrave Square, London
SW1X 8PY. The government's
conservation organization. It also
issues permits for bird
photography.

Rambler's Association, 1/4
Crawford Mews, London
W1H 1PT. Guards access to the
countryside.

**The Royal Society for Nature
Conservation,** The Green,
Nettleham, Lincolnshire.
Co-ordinates the work of the
County Trusts for Nature
Conservation, which acquire and
manage local reserves, and
organize activities.

**The Royal Society for the
Protection of Birds,** The Lodge,
Sandy, Bedfordshire. Sets up
reserves for birds, helps enforce
protection laws and organizes
research and education.

The Young Ornithologists' Club,
The Lodge, Sandy, Bedfordshire.
The junior branch of the RSPB
(members up to 15 years old).
Organizes projects and courses.

Glossary

Brood. A family of young birds. To brood is to cover the young to keep them warm.

Clutch. A full complement of eggs in the nest.

Coverts. The feathers which cover the bases of the tail and wing feathers.

Display. Any behaviour of constant form used for communication between individuals.

Down. The soft, fluffy feathers covering young birds and forming a layer under the feathers of adult birds.

Eclipse plumage. The dull plumage of some male ducks worn during the summer.

Environment. The sum of the conditions of soil, vegetation, climate etc. which affect an animal or plant.

Fledge. The acquisition, by a nestling, of feathers enabling flight.

Gape. The open mouth of a bird.

Habitat. The sort of countryside in which an animal or plant normally lives.

Incubation. The process of sitting on the eggs to keep them warm so the chicks can hatch successfully.

Invertebrate. An animal without a backbone. This includes the insects, spiders, millipedes and centipedes, worms, slugs and snails.

Iridescent. Having glittering, changing colours.

Irruption. An irregular migration.

Juvenile. A young bird, from the time it can fly until it moults its first coat of feathers.

Mollusc. A group of animals which includes the snails and slugs.

Moult. The shedding of old feathers and growth of new ones.

Moustachial stripe. A dark stripe on the face of a bird, which looks like a moustache.

Nidicolous. Describes a young bird which stays in the nest until it can fly.

Nidifugous. Describes a young bird which leaves the nest soon after hatching.

Parasitize. To live on another animal and cause it harm, eg, by taking its food.

Pesticides. Chemicals used to kill pests. They include weedkillers and insecticides.

Plumage. The entire covering of feathers.

Primary feathers. The main flight feathers, on the outer part of the wing.

Scapulars. Feathers that cover base of the wing.

Secondary feathers. Flight feathers on the inner part of the wing.

Species. A kind of animal or plant. Related species make up a family.

Speculum. A patch of brightly coloured feathers on a duck's wing.

Talon. The sharp claw of a bird of prey.

Tendon. The sinew joining a muscle to a bone.

Territory. An area defended against other members of the species. Nesting takes place here.

Index Scientific names

Index English names

PDO 82-0106